I Do, Part 2

How to Survive Divorce,
Co-Parent Your Kids,
and Blend Your Families
Without Losing Your Mind

Karen Buscemi

Printed in the United States of America

ISBN: 978-1-935254-36-2

Cover Design by NorLightsPress Graphic Department
Book Design by Nadene Carter
Author Photo by Daniel Lippitt

First printing, 2011

Dedication

For my flawed yet fully functional family—
every last one of you.

Acknowledgements

I have to thank my ex, Andrew Correll, and our spouses, Frank Buscemi and Kathy Kelley, first, because without the four of us stumbling our way through divorce, co-parenting and new friendships, there would be no book. I'm grateful for the three of you.

Thanks to my sons, Noah and Jesse, for always bringing a smile to my face, especially when there was far too much on my plate.

I thank my mom for the tons of babysitting and always asking, "How can I help?"

Big thanks to my agent Krista Goering, for shopping until she (nearly) dropped and believing in this project. A hearty thank you to my editor Sammie Justesen for being so delightful to me and always enthusiastic about this book. And a sincere thanks to Carolyn Krieger-Cohen of CKC Public Relations for getting people to pay attention to my message.

I'm grateful to my experts: Scott Haltzman, LeslieBeth Wish, Joyce Morley, and Peter Nielsen for lending their knowledge to the book.

To Leslie Ann Pilling and Janis—it was brave of you both to share your stories of divorce, and I thank you for trusting me with your histories.

And a shout out to my writer friends, Lynne Schreiber, Susan Shapiro, Claire Charlton, Stacy Duford, Maureen McDonald, Ellen Piligian, Theresa Falzone, and everyone else who took part in the writers' group and book critiques. We make a great team.

Contents

Note from the Author

*H*aving divorced my husband when our son was three, I've spent the last ten years learning how to do the post-divorce dance—successfully—and even renewed my once close friendship with my ex-mother-in-law. How did we accomplish this? Mainly, by not trying to ruin each other's lives during the divorce proceedings, giving each other time to get used to the new arrangement, reinserting humor into the relationship, and doing our best to help and respect one another. Was that all? Heck no! If it were that easy, thousands of therapists would be out of business. However, the effort we made during and after the divorce was the foundation for what is today a real friendship between my ex and me, my ex and my new husband, and my ex's new wife and me. We may sound like the exception to the rule, but the secret is—we both wanted to do whatever it took to make a good life for our son.

While I hope my personal experience will inspire and motivate you to create your own version of one big happy family, I've sprinkled in words of wisdom from experts whose wisdom comes from years of education and working with couples before, during, and after divorce. And I've provided stories, tips, and advice from divorced friends, who found their own versions of happy, mingled families.

While everyone won't become best pals with their former partner, *I Do, Part 2* will help divorced parents forge more civil relationships to benefit both sides of the family and bring the kind of peace that comes after two or three Cabernets. Or perhaps a nice syrah.

1

Getting Divorced? First Things First

*S*o, you're getting a divorce. That sucks. If it's just the two of you, I implore you to opt for the quickest, simplest divorce possible, then run—don't walk—into your new life. But if you and your almost-ex spawned a kid with *both* your DNA, get ready to say hello to a different kind of life that feels strangely familiar. Because unless your former love is moving to Antarctica to start a snowmobile business, the two of you still have many years to navigate together. You'll just be doing it from different houses. With different spouses. And maybe a few more kids. Doesn't that sound like fun?

I can't stress enough how critical the divorce itself is to the future wellbeing of your relationship. If you're picking up this book after a messy divorce, you may be thinking, "Ah, crap!" But don't panic. A less than ideal parting of the ways doesn't mean all is lost. You may need a little extra time and effort to repair and reconstruct the relationship. And now that you're a single parent learning a new role, you have plenty of extra time for re-bonding with your ex, right?

When I divorced my ex nine years ago, I didn't file for divorce until seven months after separating. Why? Because I couldn't afford an attorney right away. But my money woes actually had a positive effect on the divorce. Enough time had passed since the announcement I was moving out (Independent Me chose to find new digs, since leaving was my idea) for that initial sting to dissipate. We spent seven months stumbling through our three-year-old son Noah's custody options (we went with every other day—more on that later), learning how to help each other with scheduling conflicts (just to be nice!), and agreeing on whose wallet would get lighter and when (I'll pay for school pictures if you go to Old Navy for new underwear). By the time I was able to cough up the cash for representation, we'd already made most of the decisions a lawyer would help us sort out. We only needed someone to handle the paperwork. And so I hired one attorney for the both of us.

Ideal? Maybe. Easy? Hell No. Don't think for a minute our relationship was so ideal we high-fived in court. This was difficult and terribly uncomfortable. I never stopped feeling guilty for changing my son's simple life. Not for one minute. It was next to impossible for me to make eye contact with my ex. I'd made a decision that benefited only me (although to this day I don't regret it), and I fully understood the weight of my actions. Perhaps it was that understanding, and not having a divanistic attitude about everything I felt I deserved, that allowed us to have a Bruce and Demi divorce, before Bruce and Demi knew their relationship was on the rocks. Hiring one divorce lawyer won't be an option for everyone. There may be issues the two of you can't agree on by yourselves. Maybe the reason for your parting is more hurtful (hello, infidelity?), or you've both harbored a lot of anger for years. You may even be in a place where you can't look at your almost-ex without wanting to issue a release to the paparazzi about his or her evil ways, a la Charlie Sheen and Denise Richards. What's more important? Keeping the peace. Even if your mate left you for someone new, you have to suck it up and get through the divorce *without* punishment. No, "I'll show you!" allowed. And no being stubborn about that ugly, yet ridiculously expensive stained-glass lamp you never really liked, either. Just get through it, get what you need, and move on with your life. You'll be finding someone better when you're good and ready.

Work Out the Details Before Hiring an Attorney. Whether you're pissed off to the point that only vodka will help, or you're secretly relieved to be free, work out as many details as possible for both the divorce and custody arrangement *before* you hire a lawyer. Watching two attorneys bicker like Itchy & Scratchy is only going to make you more tense and whittle away more of your hard-earned funds, while the professionals you hired are, in fact, laughing all the way to the bank. Why should they have all the fun?

"The more agreeable you are, the less painful the divorce process will be for you," says Joyce Morely, Ed.D, a psychotherapist and relationship expert in Atlanta, who also happens to be a divorced mother of three daughters. "Be amicable. Practice respect by looking at the needs of the other while at the same time meeting your own needs. Figure out the points of contention and come to an agreement about how to divide everything: the finances, the children's time. If you can do that together, writing it all down and signing it, you can stick to one attorney."

My friend Janis' husband left after ten years of marriage. They had three young boys at the time, ages three, five, and seven. Though the divorce came as a surprise and Janis had to deal with the anxiety of wondering how she'd provide for herself and the kids while "bursting into tears at strange times," she and her ex managed to get through a civil divorce—largely because of a combination of deciding all the legal issues in advance and doing their best to be decent to one another.

"The legal part of the divorce was extremely easy," she recalls, "which was good, because I was like a deer in headlights. I didn't have to go to court. Other than signing a lot of papers in a lawyer's office, I didn't have to do anything. He was an okay guy and responsible financially, so money was taken care of between the two of us and we didn't have to deal with Friend of the Court."

Janis' big request was to stay in the house, to which her ex agreed. "I didn't want my boys having to adjust to new schools and everything else," she says. "And the community we lived in was kind and supportive to me and my kids, plus my sister lived two blocks away, so I wanted to stay there." They also decided that her ex would continue making the house payment. "The home had been in my family for many years and we got it at a bargain, so making the house payment wasn't the end of the world for him. We agreed that once the house was eventually sold, we would each get half of the profits."

Try to Solve Issues Before Going to Court. Indeed, one of the most important issues you should try to resolve before heading to court is the house: Will one person remain in the house, and if so, who? Or, will you sell it and split the profits so you both can start over in fresh surroundings? Whatever you decide to do with your abode, I beg of you, DO NOT stay in the same home until the divorce is final. That's the quickest way to find dozens of new reasons to detest each other. Everything bad that could possibly happen *will* happen. Why? Because at least one of you is feeling dejected at the moment, and watching the other go on with a different life will not go over well. This is also when couples start doing things to purposely piss off each other.

You want my stuff picked up so the house looks good for potential buyers? Say hello to wet towels on the floor, worn underwear on top of the comforter, and hair clippings strewn across the toilet seat. And what if one of you has already begun dating? You can't hide getting gussied up with an extra spray of the good-smelling stuff for a special evening. (Oh, sure, no hurt feelings there.) And nothing makes you feel guilty (or sixteen) like sneaking into your own home at 3 a.m. For the sake of post-divorce peace, one of you needs to find somewhere else to live, even if it's a college roommate's unfinished basement.

We went with selling the house and buying two smaller homes, mainly because neither of us could afford the mortgage on our larger house on our own. And I wasn't about to deal with alimony. Unless you're a stay-at-home mom/dad, work part-time because you both agreed one person should be around more often for the kids, or your ex has as much pocket cash as Jay-Z, alimony is one of those "areas" that will leave the person who's paying (84 percent of the payers are men, according to *Divorce* magazine) feeling singled out, bitter, and cheering for the other to marry anything on two legs.

Child support, of course, is a totally different subject. The kids deserve to be financially sound (and have winter coats when there's a -17 F wind chill). They should also have daycare, soccer uniforms, and everything else they had before their parents decided to split. You, on the other hand, should stay away from other people's money, if at all possible. You can slow down the rebuilding process if your ex finds out you spent alimony on a cruise for you and your new hottie. Independence is an amazing feeling. Sure, it's the harder route financially, but once you get settled into your own life with your own money, not only will you have taught your tots a valuable lesson about self-reliance, you'll also increase your chances of having a cordial relationship with your ex.

Stay Away from Blame to Lessen Hostility. The number one way to lessen hostility? Stay away from blame. "To move forward, you have to move beyond self blame, as well as blame of each other," says Morely. "That's often what gets in the way of healing." This advice makes perfect sense, but can be *so* hard to follow. Blame is what we do while showering. Blame rolls around in our heads when we can't drift off to sleep at night. It plays constantly between our ears while we're stuck in a traffic jam, and comes to mind virtually every time something reminds us of the divorce. Whether you're blaming yourself or dropping it all on your ex's head, placing blame—a natural impulse when you're in the thick of divorce—is what keeps us angry, pent up, and a candidate for high blood pressure. While blame may feel all good and powerful for a little while (yes, pointy finger, I'm talking to you), in the end you just make yourself feel crappy. Because blame, no matter whom it's directed at, means you haven't let go.

My friend Leslie has been divorced twice, and though they were completely different divorces in terms of how they ended, she managed to reach friendly situations with both her exes. She married ex number one at twenty-two and divorced seven years later. Their son, who was four at the time, is now twenty-six.

"We mutually decided to get divorced," she says of the first marriage. "I can only say great things about him and he's a great daddy. The marriage just didn't continue. It was time and we still remain friends."

She was married to ex number two for ten years. Their son was three at the time of the divorce and is now thirteen. And though the divorce was rougher—she says she initiated it and he didn't take it well—thanks to the relationship she developed with her ex's new wife, the situation with him improved over the years.

"We still have rocky moments," she says about ex number two, "but the relationship has stabilized in its own right. The difference is, I used to give him permission to push buttons, and now I don't give him permission. I'm more calm about it."

Her trick for keeping the relationship stable post-divorce is to see it more as a business relationship. "I think that's a great way for people to handle things," she says. "You know you need certain things done; you know the smart way to accomplish things, and that's what you go for."

She received alimony and child support from ex number one and just child support from ex number two.

"I think it's important to split things," she says. "This is about equality. One needs to take care of the other. That's the bottom line."

It's Possible to Become Friends Again. If your divorce did go bad, and you can't get yourself to therapy (or, the bar) fast enough, fear not. It is possible to be civil—and even (gasp!) become friends once again. This is true even if your ex is resentful, holding a grudge, and/or talking negatively about you to the postal carrier and the UPS guy. It only takes one person to make a bad situation better. And since you're the one reading this book, you're going to have to step up and start the repair process. Changes will take time, but your kindness, respect and understanding (yes, you will need all three— feel free to lay down for a bit and process that), will chip away at your ex's bitterness until that person you once liked begins to reappear. You may not have made a good marriage, but you still have a chance to be good friends. Okay, maybe just friends. Or at least good parents, who get along.

Leslie Beth Wish, Ed.D., MSS, a psychologist, licensed clinical social worker, and founder of lovevictory.com, who also writes a weekly Relationship Realities column for qualityhealth.com, suggests beginning to break down animosity by writing your ex a sincere letter.

Consider Wish's example below for your first draft:

Dear Ex, (Please don't refer to your ex as Ex. This is just a placeholder. Let's not piss off anyone when we're just getting started.)

We have made a wonderful child together. I'm sorry it didn't work out, from the bottom of my heart. You have wonderful qualities. I wish you happiness in your life. I want to be friends. For the sake of our child, I know we can work together. Not on everything—I respect your differences—but on important things. I hope you feel comfortable coming to me, and I hope you'll make it comfortable for me to come to you. Thank you for our wonderful child.

So, how do you start the rebuilding process? Carefully.

My friend Janis says kindness and acceptance played a huge role in getting through her divorce and learning how to parent together as exes.

"It is what it is," she says. "Divorce is a crushing thing. What's the point of rehashing hurts? Just accept that it's over, maybe you at least learned something from it, and move ahead and try to be a decent person."

Leslie's advice came straight from her mom. "She told me to always be cordial, polite, and a lady. So I do my best."

I know it sounds like a tall order, trying to break through to someone who'd rather watch a *Whose Wedding Is It Anyway?* marathon than be in the same room with you. But it can be done. Like I said, it's all about kindness, respect, and understanding: A whole lot of it. And did I mention patience? You'll know the struggle was worth it when the two of you are shooting friendly emails back and forth regarding Junior's summer camp schedule. So, are you ready to get started? Then let's go:

The Dos and Don'ts of Breaking Through After Breaking Up

DO

1. Speak to your ex in a friendly, yet not overly animated tone. You don't want to give the impression you're having the time of your life now that you're single.

2. Return phone calls and emails in a timely manner without ever saying, "What now?"

3. Agree to any schedule changes that don't honestly send your day into chaos. If you can make it happen, do it.

4. Drop off and pick up your kid at the agreed upon time. If you can do the switch at your homes, instead of say, the parking lot at KFC, the process will feel less cold.

5. Pick up that book your kid needs for school without noting, "Don't forget I paid for his Mohawk, too."

6. Ask before taking anything from your shared house—if you're not living there. If it's yours, it's yours, but respect boundaries by getting permission before entering the home.

7. Speak kindly about your ex to your kid. This is not the time to introduce your little one to new curse words.

8. Keep your ex abreast of Junior's updates: grades, mood swings, girlfriends, girlfriends with mood swings. Keeping each other in the loop means no surprises.

9. Be courteous. When your ex agrees to change the schedule so you can go out with your friends, say thank you. If your ex comments your stomach looks surprisingly less blubbery, *just* say thank you.

10. Remember you're the good example you hope your ex will one day become. Unless your former flame has a voodoo doll in your image and has taken to muttering your name repeatedly under a local bridge, your positive energy *will* have a positive effect.

DON'T

1. Hug, pat on the back, or fondle your ex in any way whatsoever. Experiencing that jolt of electricity from your touch is going to set you way, way back.

2. Roll your eyes or sigh if your ex breaks down and cries in your presence. Remain still and wait for it to pass.

3. Post your sexual conquests on your MySpace page. In fact, question why you have a MySpace page.

4. Allow your new love to answer your phone. Ever.

5. Fill your youngster with caffeinated beverages and cupcakes before dropping him off to your ex. If you can't handle him bouncing off the walls, neither can anyone else.

6. Wear your wedding ring on your right hand because "it looks nice."
7. Reminisce about the good times, unless it's specifically about your kid. Nobody wants to be reminded how much fun it *was* to be together.
8. Try to look your best every time you see your ex. Show you care by not showering or using deodorant for a few days.
9. Drive past your ex's house for curiosity's sake. Even if you need to travel down that street to reach your destination, find another route.
10. Initially move in with anyone who isn't the same sex as you, unless you moved out because you're gay.

2

A Custody Agreement You Can Live With

*I*t's difficult enough deciding what to wear each day or what ice cream flavor to order. How do you determine something as critical as your kid's daily life? For some ex-couples, this is a no brainer: Dad works too many hours, so Mom gets primary custody. Or Mom had a midlife crisis and is sunning herself on a boat by day and hitting the clubs at night, leaving Dad as the caregiver. Yet for many, custody isn't so cut and dried. Both parents may be entertaining thoughts of days upon days of quality one-on-one time with Junior (also known as an irreconcilable scenario that screams "custody battle"). And while splitting the time equally is a fair option, you can find more than one way to accomplish that. Do you want to try an every other day arrangement? Perhaps two-day blocks of time? While it might seem simpler to flip a coin for custody, a more sensible option is to consider various arrangements, basing your final decision on schedules, locations, and what's best for Baby.

Joint Custody (Physical and Legal)

Unless you've got a nice trust fund in place, you and your ex probably work outside the home, making your schedules equally busy. And if those jobs include travel or after-hours functions, finding that "quality time" (read: three games of Nintendo Wii Bowling) for a child can be a heck of a challenge. However, if joint custody is what you had in mind, be sure you can make the time to do school pickups, monitor homework, and get your wee one to soccer practice with something semi-nutritional in his belly.

If you're lucky enough to have outside support from your own parents, or perhaps a sibling living nearby, you may be able to work out an agreement with them to help out with driving or after-school care. (If you've been distant from said relatives, this is the time to start sucking up—and fast.) Many schools have before- and after-care programs for a fee that is well worth the money.

I don't know what I would have done without before care and after care. I took full advantage of both, and the programs were so fun, filled with dodge ball, art projects, and computer games, that my son, Noah would bring out the severely depressed face if I dropped him off too late to play for a little while before school. His face was equally tragic on the few occasions when I left work early and picked him up as the bell rang, quashing his kickball plans. Before care and after care allows you to get to work on time in the morning and stay late for that mandatory impromptu meeting, never having to worry about Junior's whereabouts. For the busy single parent, it's as good as gold. (Almost.)

Joint physical and legal custody means not only does your kid live at both your houses, you and your ex are also responsible for making joint decisions regarding your youngster's life. This is yet another reason to learn to live in harmony: having a good parenting relationship means selecting a new pediatrician or determining the age your little pride and joy can get his tongue pierced without it resulting in f-bombs and name calling.

Coming up with a joint custody arrangement depends not only on your schedule, but also on your personality. I wanted an every-other day arrangement, because it allowed me to see my son every day of the week, even if it was a hurried morning of teeth brushing, vitamin popping, and a frazzled drive to school. Though rushed and chaotic, we still manage real one-on-one time I would never give up. I also secretly didn't want him at his dad's too many days in a row for fear he would like it better and want to stay permanently. Nine years later, we're still following the same schedule, with no complaints from anyone, even Noah. The marriage may not have lasted, but it appears the custody arrangement will be in place until death do us part (or college comes along).

My friend Janis and her ex had a joint custody arrangement whereby the bulk of parenting—and time spent with the kids—were her responsibility. She had her boys most every night, with her ex taking them one evening during the week and for an overnight almost every weekend. She says that during their marriage, he was busy with his career and often came home after the kids were in bed anyway, so it wasn't much of a change after the divorce. And this didn't affect the kids either, since they were already used to the situation.

Sometimes, You Need More Time. If you're not into the constant back and forth or could use a larger block of alone time, consider two- or three-day arrangements. Example: you take Sunday through Tuesday, your ex takes Wednesday through Friday, and you each get half of Saturday. Fair, square, and you each get one weekend night free.

Another option is one week on, one week off. This is a good arrangement if you suck at juggling and prefer longer blocks of time to bond with your kid. This scenario is *not* ideal, however, if you regularly push off the undesirable parenting tasks on your ex: toenail clipping, pulling out that wiggly tooth, bathing. If you've got your kid all week, you have no choice but to deal with all the down and dirty deeds—no matter how grossed out you may be. (And no, that is *not* a reason to get remarried.) Seriously though, make sure you can handle a whole week without your pride and joy. That week of no parenting at first may sound liberating, but you could quickly find yourself puttering around the house in a ratty sweater, missing your son's twenty-minute-long stories, or braiding your cat's fur because your daughter isn't around. Thankfully, in a world of camera phones and video conferencing, you're never that far away from the one you love.

My friend Leslie has joint custody with both exes and worked out a week on-week off custody arrangement for both her kids. And while the first custody arrangement was mutually decided and easy to set up, the second was a much greater challenge that included a separate attorney to handle a parenting agreement.

"We needed representation from the child's point of view," she explains. "I wanted my ex to be an active parent, so we needed something in writing." The parenting agreement covers everything from safety issues, such as wearing a helmet while riding a bike, to the schedule and holidays, to handling medical issues. And she says since the agreement went into effect, the improvement on her ex's part "has been huge."

Sole Custody

Though it's not a fun reality, you may have a situation where, for the good of your kid, you need to have sole custody. From a serious addiction to just being a workaholic, if your ex is unable to care for your kid, the responsibility falls in your lap.

This is a tough time to be worrying about becoming buddies with your ex, when what's really on your mind is probably a satisfying fantasy consisting of your ex, a cliff, and you winning the lottery the next day. Still, if you want a peaceful future and a well-adjusted kid, you need to keep that long-term, harmonious partnership in mind.

Your ex may or may not get some type of visitation rights—that's likely up to the courts—but either way, you have a job to keep your kid and his other parent connected and communicating. If there is no visitation, encourage both to use photos, video, email, cards—whatever it takes to maintain the parent-kid relationship. If visitation is granted, get your kid excited to hang out with your ex by talking enthusiastically about the visits. Stay positive, keep the experience upbeat, and then, if the situation ever changes and your ex is in a good place to share custody, you've already laid the groundwork for affable co-parenting.

Location, Location, Location

Where you live plays a big factor in the time you spend with your kid. Obviously, if you have joint custody, you need to live somewhat near your ex, otherwise shuffling Junior back and forth is going to suck—a lot. And then imagine if he forgets something at one of his houses. (Mine does at least three times a week. *After* he's been reminded not to forget.) Even though it might sound nice to move to a new town where everyone you pass on the street doesn't say, "Poor thing, how are you holding up?" it will benefit everyone involved if you keep within a fifteen-minute drive of each other's homes.

I moved around a bit after my divorce, and finally settled eight miles from my ex. Let me tell you, it was too far away. It sounded perfect—really only one city away—but that was exactly far enough to be annoying. Meanwhile, my ex moved a few blocks away from our son's school, so he got to wave bye-bye from the front door as Noah pedaled his bike to school, while I had to schlep Noah, my baby Jesse, and all their stuff into the car, through morning traffic, and then unload Jesse once we were back home. I had been doing the forty-minute round-trip drive for four years (one with the baby), and you know what? That got old. Quick. I finally convinced my husband Frank to sell our house so by the time Noah started high school we'd only be a few blocks away. Know what we did instead? We fell in love with a house and neighborhood roughly nine miles away from my ex. And that's where we live now. Nobody said we were the smartest bananas in the bunch when it comes to convenience of location. Now we're counting down the days until Noah can drive. (1,215 days to go!)

Of course, you won't always have the option to live exactly where you want. Maybe your ex has a famous movie producer father who decided to bestow his grown child a sprawling ranch in an upscale neighborhood. (Post-divorce. Figures.) Maybe you thought it would be a great idea to move in with your mother (sorry!) for awhile to save money. If you can't live nearby, you want to think about what's realistic with your custody agreement, especially where Junior's school and friends are concerned.

While the divorce is most likely tough for you, it's even tougher for your kid, so if you don't have to pull him out of school and away from his friends, don't. Do whatever you can to maintain stability in his life. That's why I do the crappy drive. Noah had been in the same public school system since preschool, and I wasn't about to have him change schools just because I wanted to live in a different city. I'm torturing the kid enough, making him transport dirty diapers upstairs to the baby's Diaper Genie. A new school, too? That would just be cruel.

If you're living, say forty-five minutes from your kid's school, can you really commit to getting him back and forth, including after-school activities? Noah gets out of school just after three and has to be at soccer practice twice a week at six. And, wouldn't you know, the soccer field is even further from my house than his school. The timing is spaced out enough that my only choice is to drive Noah home after school, have him do homework and eat dinner, then load him and his smelly soccer bag back into the car for the even more annoying drive to soccer. Which lasts an hour and a half. Did I mention how much better it is to live near your kid's school? If you're trying to do what's best for your kid and you live too far away to get him where he needs to be, having him stay with you during the week may not be practical. If you're not willing to do a weekend-only arrangement, be sure to choose a home in a reasonable location.

Improve Your Flexibility

This is not an aside on the importance of yoga—although in the case of divorce, knowing how to relax your body and calm your mind certainly is a desirable ability. (More on that in Chapter 5.) I'm talking about flexible schedules, why they're important, and why they can be more difficult than an hour of non-stop Sun Salutations.

As I mentioned before, my ex and I have an every other day custody arrangement. It basically breaks down to me having Noah Monday, Wednesday, Friday; his dad, Tuesday, Thursday, Saturday, and then we each take part of Sunday.

But that's not where it ends.

Only having our kid half the time, neither of us are thrilled with the idea of having someone babysit him if we have an evening engagement. That night out of the house means I only get to tuck Noah into bed two days out of the week, which does not work for me. Therefore, at the beginning of every week, his dad and I chat via phone or email to go over our schedules and decide if anything needs to be changed. Generally, it doesn't. We know our schedules and we try our best to stick to them, scheduling cocktails and all that other good adult stuff on the nights we're on our own. However, it's inevitable that something will come up to pull one of us away on a day with our boy. Then our conversation goes something like this:

"Can you switch Tuesday-Wednesday this week?"

"Pretty sure. I was going to ask if you could switch Friday-Saturday, since (new wife's son) will be at his dad's, and (new wife) and I can actually go out without the kids."

"That works. Make sure you email this conversation to me or I'll forget by tomorrow."

It's that easy-going. Of course we can't always help each other out with the schedule. That's where family members and babysitters come into play. But if we can, we do. Why act put out or insist on sticking to a strict schedule when, after those little dramas we sometimes like to create are set aside, making such a minute change has no major impact on our lives whatsoever? Plus this way, when it's my turn to ask for help, I know I'm going to get it. And my ex won't make me feel guilty about it either. And believe me, it doesn't take much to make me feel guilty.

"When you're flexible, you build a reserve pot," says Morely. "When you need something the next time, your ex will be more willing, because you were willing, too." She also notes that besides being good for your new divorced relationship, it's good for your kid. "It models positively for the child," Morely says, "to see communication and respect between parents."

You and your ex might find some other scheduling method that better suits you both—there's no single solution—and as long as you're both doing your best to make life easier for one another, you're on the right track. This is one of the first, and also the most important, spots in your divorce where you both can start the work toward becoming allies, and eventually friends. If that sounds like too much to swallow so soon, then think of it as working toward not killing each other. Whatever works for the moment.

Money, Money, Money

Part of the custody agreement includes figuring out who pays for the cajillion things your kid needs: clothing, doctor appointment co-pays, sports uniforms, summer camp, tutoring, books, school lunch, birthday party presents, day care, before/after care, field trips, teacher presents—and the list goes on and on.

This, naturally, will be based on both of your incomes. If one person makes substantially more than the other, that's going to make a difference in who pays for what. My ex was making a hell of a lot more than me when we divorced, so we agreed he would handle day care, the most expensive item on the list at the time, and we'd split everything else. Once Noah was old enough for school, his dad's day care money went to the before- and after-care program. Each season, we have Noah try on all his clothes to see what still fits (usually, very little), and then we divide the clothing purchases. I might handle pants, underwear, and shoes, while he buys shirts, socks and the winter coat.

Figuring out the money situation (which can be adjusted in the future as finances change), as well as custody, is something you want to do *without* the help of the courts, if at all possible. The justice system may be trying to do what's best for the kid, but as long as you and your ex are being levelheaded about your divorce decisions, you two know best what everyone involved needs. Get everything agreed upon before you hire the attorney(s) and you'll save time, money, and tons of aggravation.

Determining custody for your child is, of course, a huge decision, but bear in mind the arrangement *is* changeable. You may feel you're not getting enough time with your kid (or not enough time alone), or your set days have become a conflict because of a new job or some other valid reason. The point is, custody is not set in stone. Do give it some time—it may just take getting settled into a new routine—but if you find the arrangement you've got isn't turning out to be the arrangement you thought it would be, consider new options, keep building a good relationship with your ex, take lots of bubble baths (guys like to have silky skin, too), then work out a new solution.

3

Parenting Styles

$\mathcal{A}$h, parenting. Amazing how this one enormous responsibility, broken down into a multitude of tasks, headaches, and crying sessions, not only comes with no manual (until I write one, of course), but also has every parent eventually convinced he or she has it all figured out. Things are complex enough when you're married and your parenting style doesn't mirror your spouse's. For instance, in my current marriage I have a big don't-rile-up-the-baby-before-bedtime policy, while my husband thinks jammies is code for basketball shoot-outs and rousing games of tag. Needless to say, I have a large repertoire of eye rolls in my arsenal when the baby is too hyper to go to sleep. There's a good cop and a bad cop in every marriage—or at least a sort-of-cool cop and a kind-of-unfair cop. When you're under the same roof, it's a little easier to deal with parenting differences, because the mom or dad with stricter homework rules and curfew restrictions is going to break through the muddle and see to it the kid is towing the line. When you're parenting from separate houses with different styles, however, a kid can get some seriously mixed signals—and you and your ex can drive each other to drink. (Or, to drink more.) To keep your bar bill low, your gray hairs at bay, and your relationship with your ex at peace, you've got to come to an agreement on a few basic rules for your kid.

Punishment

Whether they are two or twelve, kids are going to break the rules, and punishments will need to be doled out. However you choose to handle it, this has to be a mutual decision you both carry out. To term. (I'm talking to you, Good Cop.) Here's the thing: divorce is like a magic pill that makes kids instantly crafty. They figure out ways to work their parents over so we feel guilty (as if we didn't already feel that in spades) or neglectful, or worse, at risk of becoming the less-favored parent. What better way to make up for all our wrongdoings than to look the other way when Junior misses his curfew or fails a test? But that's exactly why it's so important for you and your ex to stand firm on the rules—and what happens when rules are broken; because your kid is going to test you now more than ever, and you have to show him that just because his parents are busy navigating new lives, you're not about to stop governing his.

If you already have good discipline rules in place from when you were still married, agree to continue with them, adjusting as your kid gets older. (You've got to know what's going to hurt most when you confiscate it.) And whatever the term is for the punishment, see it through. That will keep his behavior consistent from one house to the other.

If you establish new punishment rules, be sure you keep track of what they are and how long they last. An amazing invention known as GoogleDocs is perfect for keeping track of anything related to your kid. All you have to do is set up an account, create simple documents or spreadsheets with titles such as: Noah's Punishment Guide, Noah's Current Punishments, What Will Keep Noah From Ever Getting His Own Car (you get the idea), and give each other access to the documents via an email address. A Google calendar will let you share important dates, such as the length of current punishment, as well as things like vacation days, birthday parties, soccer games— you name it. If by chance you're reading this book twenty-five years from the publication date (good material circulates a *long* time) and Google has become as antiquated as leisure suits, I'm sure there's an even better system available for tracking punishments. Take it upon yourself to find it and start using it.

Homework

Depending on your kid, homework can be an easy topic, or it can bring you inches from fingerprinting and a mug shot. With mine it's the latter. He's a good boy. A wonderfully funny, sensitive kid. But when it comes to homework, he's hell on wheels, or at least a pain in my backside with a backpack. Micromanagement is the only way to ensure assignments are completed *and* turned in (the turning in part is often the most difficult task). And don't even get me started on studying for tests. Each day after arriving home from school, his excuses are already lined up for why he can't get right to his homework: exhaustion, extreme hunger, a taped repeat of Two and a Half Men. (Our DVR is usually at 98 percent capacity, so he believes he's doing me a favor by watching his shows so he can delete them, thus freeing up space for me.) And then there are legitimate homework interferences, such as soccer practices and jazz band rehearsals. Needless to say, keeping him focused is a two-person job.

As if you can't tell already, let me assure you, I am Bad Cop. His dad is more the wannabe bad cop who can be coerced to look the other way. Okay, not so much coerced as at a donut shop enjoying the tasty goodness of a fresh Bavarian cream and forgetting to keep a close eye on his ward. The point is, it's easy for exes to argue—and the kid's academics may suffer in the process—if only one parent is actually parenting diligently, especially where schoolwork is concerned. That means you need to establish a system to keep tabs on assignments, quizzes and tests, conferences, and the dreaded progress reports.

Now you may have an angel, who strives to get all A's and mentally beats himself up if he gets a B+ in his toughest subject. To you I say, feel free to skip this section of the chapter, and I'm very resentful of you. Not only do I not have that kind of a kid, I also have a boy. If you have a son you're already nodding your head, because for most of us that means dealing with a level of disorganization that only escalates when he has to move his backpack—and all the papers slip from his binders into the great unknown—from house to house. And I'm not generalizing or stereotyping the boys. I read an article a couple of years ago in The New York Times regarding boys and issues with disorganization and time management. It felt good to know my son isn't the only one. But it also means my ex and I must be diligent and follow the same parenting rules. Most of the time, anyway.

We made sure Noah had one of those big binders with compartments and sections for each subject. And his assignment book was clipped in there too. The more we could get everything in a single place—even down to his pens and student ID—the better. Even if he doesn't always have everything filed properly, as long as it's all in there, we can find what we need to see on any given day and then assign him a weekend project to give the binder a good weeding.

We check his assignment book every day, and then verify each assignment is completed and inside the binder pocket assigned to it. That's really the worst of the organization part. The other crucial element is for my ex and I to communicate with each other regarding school issues. This is usually just a heads up, generally via email, to let the other know there's a problem. Be it a missing assignment (very common with Noah), a bad grade on a test, or an overall slumping grade in a subject. The next step is usually a punishment to get him back on track. For instance, if he has any missing assignments during the week, he can't get together with his friends over the weekend. If he gets a bad grade on a test, he loses his iPod for a week. We figure this out with an email exchange, keeping consistent with how we punish. Whoever he's with that night gets the pleasure of doling out the punishment, with hand held out to capture the oft-confiscated iPod. See that? Who says there's no fun after divorce?

The Other Stuff

Once you've got punishments and homework all figured out and into practice, it's time to move on to other areas where you and your ex need to be on board the same parenting train so Junior knows exactly what's expected, no matter which house he's currently decorating with dirty clothes, wet towels, and strings of headphones. (Dear Apple and all your third party vendors: How many sets of headphones does one kid need?) Oh yeah, I was making a list here:

- Bedtime routine
- Chores
- Allowance
- Mealtime
- Curfew
- Video games and computers
- Presents
- Parties
- Sleepovers
- Play dates
- Dating

Agreeing on the rules for these various areas—and sticking to them—will keep you and your ex on good parenting terms, and do great things for your kid in the process.

"Children crave attention from their parents, and one of the healthiest ways we can provide attention is setting clear limits with them, and being able to give them feedback about their success or failure in meeting our expectations," says Scott Haltzman, MD, a Distinguished Fellow of the American Psychiatric Association and medical director of NRI Community Services in Woonsocket, Rhode Island, who has been happily married for 22 years (sure, rub it in). "Children actually fear having too much freedom, and may be driven by anxiety to test the limits. We often feel like we are being the bad guy by telling our children they can't do something, or insisting they do something they don't want to do. In the short run, surely it will cause a lot of headaches, but over time this will improve your relationship with your child."

Learn to Compromise (and Be Okay With it). Remember that sometimes you may be faced with having to (gasp!) compromise on one—or more—of these rules, be it the parameters of the rule or how you punish when that rule is broken. I still haven't figured out why I can't make the rules for every facet of my life no matter who else is concerned, but since that only happens about 1/100th of the time, I've had to learn to say okay to ideas that aren't 100 percent all right with me. It's a lesson on lessening my grip, even where my kid is concerned. While it's not my preference, being flexible is part of surviving post-divorce child rearing. And it will bring you one step closer to the all-family soccer game where you and your ex are spotted high-fiving when Junior gets a goal.

What if your ex refuses to play by the rules? The first thing Haltzman says to ask yourself is, "Whose rules are they?"

"One of the most common reasons an ex-spouse doesn't follow rules is because he or she doesn't believe in them," explains Haltzman. "Even if you agreed on it together, more than likely you had a specific agenda the other simply capitulated to. If your ex is not following the rules, the best thing to do is ask how he or she feels about the rules, and whether it makes sense to renegotiate what was, to this point, written in stone."

While it's better for Junior to be governed by an appropriate system set forth by both of his parents, you can't force your ex to stick to the same curfew or amount of video game play allowed per day.

Wish suggests you pick your battles carefully. "It depends on how contentious your relationship is. Or how cooperative your ex-partner is," Wish notes. "Figure out what's most important to you." She also advises talking to your kid about different rules in different houses. "You need to sit down with your child and say, 'This is difficult. You're going to be living in two different worlds, and if there's any way I can help you, you let me know. But these are the rules in this house.' Don't be afraid to set limits."

If the practice in question isn't causing real harm to your kid, there isn't much you can do about it, other than let your ex know (calmly, sanely, and succinctly) that you disagree with an area of his or her parenting and why. Stay the course with the rules you believe in and make sure your kid understands the reasons for your particular rules. There's no heading into court to discuss personal differences with the judge, so make the best of it without going into battle.

My friend Leslie has similar parenting styles with ex number one, but when it comes to ex number two, they couldn't be farther apart.

"I'm much more strict," she says of her parenting style. "I need to know what my son is doing socially, who he's doing it with, and where they're going. My ex isn't like that."

She says to this day she still questions ex number two's decisions for their son. "Do I like it? No, and though I do speak up, I also have to let go," she says. "I can't have control over everything. I hope I've instilled enough common sense and patterns of choices in my son that he feels safe and knows he's making good choices."

One summer, after being divorced for a few years, my friend Janis decided to take a driving trip to California, sans kids, for two weeks. In order to stay away for so long, her ex—who generally never had the boys for more than a night at a time—had to step up and be a full-time dad for 14 days nonstop. She says he "cautiously agreed," and while there were no catastrophes while in their dad's care, Janis does point out that her youngest had to sleep in the bathtub (with proper sheets and blankets, of course), since there weren't enough beds to go around.

"That probably wasn't the way some people would think it should be handled, but they were safe," she says. "They were with their dad."

~~~~

I want to include a rule in this "other" section, because I think it's helped my ex and I have good feelings for each other throughout the ten years since our divorce: Parent Presents. Since we first separated, my ex and I have always made sure Noah had a present purchased, wrapped, and ready to go—with card—for each parent's birthday, Mother's Day/Father's Day, and Christmas. (Comic strip wrapping paper, a bag wound tight with masking tape—it wasn't always pretty, but a little effort is better than no effort, right?) We've kept the budget small—only $25—enough for Noah to find something sweet, useful, or whatever he wanted the gift to be at any particular age. We do request gift ideas from each other to make the process easier. And in the end, Noah feels great about handing his parents presents that included his involvement. He sees his parents actively trying to do something nice for each other, and we get to receive something special from our kid.

If your ex was never all that great at remembering special dates when you were married, don't expect any major breakthroughs now that you're divorced. Instead, take on the role of the reminder. Make sure those dates (both yours and your ex's) are noted in a big, bold font on your shared Internet calendar. Send an email reminder at least two weeks out. And include gift suggestions if it's your special day that's approaching. Make the process as easy as possible for the best results possible. You may encounter a speed bump now and again, and it may irritate you that you're forever having to remind your ex Christmas is only five days away, but be diligent. And calm. Keep the process about the fun. Try to use humor when your ex is slacking off (not the biting, sarcastic kind, as much as you may want to), and Parent Presents can (eventually) become an enjoyable tradition for all of you. I think it's a great way to make your kid feel that, even though his parents are no longer together, you're all part of a larger family.

4

Smiles, Everyone, Smiles

*T*hank God for girlfriends. When I first separated from my ex, they gave me everything from a place to sleep to countless rounds of beers. They were my support system and my confidants. They listened with sympathetic ears when I waxed poetic all night long about soul mates—and whose bullshit idea that was—and they put up with me once I was back in the dating game, as I nodded enthusiastically at their stories while I rubber necked every good-looking male who walked past me.

Whether you're a man or a woman going through a divorce (or still reeling from one), the one vital thing you can do to preserve any remnants of sanity is to turn to those select few trustworthy friends and start talking. If you're missing this kind of friendship from your life, then go out in pursuit of it. Rekindle a relationship with a sibling or long-lost cousin. Facebook your best friend from middle school. Find a therapist or support group. Get to know the sweet lady who has been living next door to you for the last fifteen years. Tell your dad he's not the schmuck you thought he was and book a fishing trip for two. Bottom line: find at least one confidant and enlighten that person with every good, bad, or slightly kinky detail from your courtship, your marriage, and your divorce that you need to work through. Because somebody needs to hear it and that person should never, ever, be your kid.

"It's important for your child to maintain positive feelings and a healthy alliance with each of his parents," says Haltzman. "Anytime a parent puts down his or her ex, it can be quite hurtful to a child."

Remember being a youth, when you bounded out of bed in the morning without grabbing your lower back in a fit of pain? When thinning hair was only an idea on an informercial, fixed with dark goo from a spray can? When love was the sweetest sensation, filled with endless possibilities of happily ever after? Well, they aren't called the good old days for nothing. Childhood is supposed to be magical. Santa is supposed to fit through your chimney. And kids aren't supposed to know their fathers are assholes or their mothers are lazy fat asses. And yet kids still get clued in on every negative feeling and attribute, because parents often see their youngsters as readily available sounding boards. I promise you, if they still can't erase the revolting visual of you and your ex having sex (everybody accidently walks in on it at one time or another), they certainly aren't going to be able to forget all the damaging things you declare about your ex, especially at the height of your divorce.

"A child needs an opportunity to be a child," says Morely. "Talk with your friends—don't saddle the child with that burden. Otherwise the child begins to get into self-blame. Take your issues and put them on the shoulders of someone who is stronger; who can give you some resolution. Your child doesn't need to hear sordid details about your divorce or deal with adult problems."

My friend Leslie sought out the support of friends, her mom, and her siblings while going through both divorces. But during the second divorce, she found herself talking about things with her oldest son, who was around twenty at the time. "It probably wasn't a good idea, but I would vent to him once in a while," she admits. "It's true."

Keep a Sweet Tongue. Believe me, I know how easy it can be to casually toss out a sarcastic or pissy comment with my kid in the room. My ex is famous for being late—I'm the complete opposite, of course, arriving at every appointment at least five minutes early—and it drives me freaking crazy to wait and wait and wait for my son to finally show up at my house. Or worse, when his tardiness makes me late, too. It also rattles me when my ex doesn't pay close enough attention to Noah's schoolwork and our kid ends up with a bad grade as a result. Mind you, I'm well aware these are minor things in the big picture of divorce. He could be doing *way* worse. Way, way worse. But that doesn't mean his idiosyncrasies irritate me any less. Who gets under your skin worse than those you are closest to? Nobody. And at one time, no one was closer to you than your ex. So of course you'd like to whip up a couple double-decker muscle sandwiches and hand them out. Or say something sarcastic, sadistic, sanctimonious (enter your own S word here) about your kid's other parent. The less-perfect parent. But if you do, in five, ten, or twenty years from now, only one person will still remember all the rotten things that spewed forth from your mouth. Your kid. While you've moved on and are fully enjoying the next chapter of your life, Junior will be in his own relationship, wondering if it's all worth it, and not wanting to know the pain and anger you once experienced. Or how much one person can detest another. Or be the cause of someone else's angst and bitterness.

I'm not suggesting you should paint divorce as a wondrous trip to Disneyland. It certainly is good for kids to know divorce is a painful process. Hopefully it will encourage them to think twice before entering into marriage (when they are around age thirty-four, and we've had a chance to save a couple of bucks for the reception). And hopefully it will make them aware the risk is worth taking for the chance at a rewarding life with another person. Knowledge is power, people.

So use your friends. Be a great, big user. It's the least you can do for your kids.

However.

There does come a time—once you've truly moved on and can speak from experience that is now bitter free (yes, it *will too* happen) —where you will have valuable insight to share with your kid. Your much-older kid, that is. When he is at the age where he could actually use a little advice. (Read: out of diapers, out of grade school, and out of patience with his friends' unproven counsel.) Everyone learns something from divorce. Whether it's not getting married because everyone *else* thinks you should; or why partnering with someone who doesn't share your most important values generally backfires; you have a wealth of knowledge that can help your kid avoid the mistakes you made while benefitting from the lessons you learned. So don't be afraid to take a few notes as those brilliant a-ha moments find their way into your brain. Maybe one day you can present Junior with a "Top Ten Ways to Make a Happy Marriage" list followed by "Top Ten Ways to Screw it up Big Time." Use your experiences to help ensure someone else's happiness. You might as well use it for something.

Actually, not bitching about your ex in front of your kid is the easy part. The hard part? Not fighting with your ex/soon-to-be-ex in front of Junior.

Put Down Your Dukes. We all know divorce is messy, to say the least. There are probably three couples in the entire universe (it's possible I just made up that number in order to make my point), who looked lovingly at each other over the dinner table one night and said in unison, "This isn't working out. How about we divorce, but always stay really, really great friends?" For the rest of us, divorce more likely started with a noticed distance, harsh words, or found evidence—something hurtful that got the process rolling. So, at least one set of feelings has been hurt, possibly two. And even if you were never big fighters before, chances are pretty good you're both quickly learning how to tangle. Because emotions are running high. Simply put, it's impossible not to argue a little. More likely you're arguing *a lot*. And then you look down and see your sweet little kid standing there, bawling his eyes out because his mommy and daddy can't stop yelling at each other. And so you have to find another way to release your emotions that doesn't involve scaring the hell out of your kid.

When we were divorcing, my ex was very, very hurt. I hated how much I was hurting him because he didn't do anything wrong. What I hated even more? Seeing how my then two-year-old son could feel his father's hurt, clinging to his dad like he was trying to protect him. Ten years later I can still see that scene and it makes me feel ill to know how that little kid, who was truly too young to understand any of it, intuitively recognized someone he loved was in pain.

Here's the kicker: Fighting in front of the kids—under normal circumstances, that is—is actually good for them. It's good for them to understand that arguments are a part of marriage, and Mom and Dad still love each other and will come to some sort of understanding or compromise and move on from the fight.

"Parents have disagreements," says Morely. "As long as they aren't screaming at each other or name calling, they're teaching their child that people can agree to disagree or compromise with respect."

Once again, I'm talking about a rational fight, where no one is screaming, "I wish I was dead!" or "Look what I've become because of you!" No dishes have sailed across the room, and no one's mother has been dragged into the dispute. A rational argument. Heated, without progressing into a Dynasty-esque tirade. With a divorce fight, the word "rational" has been ripped from both of your dictionaries and you're thinking how great it would be if you could administer an Alexis Carrington Colby face slap to dramatically make your point.

Repeat after me: There is no rational in divorce. Good. Therefore, the rules for fighting in front of Junior have to change. Here's the plan:

State Your Desire Not to Fight About the Divorce in Front of Your Kid. This is an important conversation and you want your soon-to-be-ex on common ground with you, so the words you choose are critical. This is most definitely *not* the time to place blame, use harsh language, or try to guilt. Calmly explain your main concern is to negatively affect your kid as little as possible.

Consider Couples Counseling. Even though reconciliation isn't an option, counseling is a safe place where the two of you can work out your hurt and anger and create a mutual plan for your future—sans divorce lawyers and judges and spending way more money than the cost of couples counseling (which may be covered by your insurance).

If One of You is too Hurt to Handle Seeing the Other, Stay Away from Each Other, at Least for a While. While it may be impossible not to see each other when dropping off or picking up your kid, make that unbelievably awkward moment quick: have Junior all packed with everything waiting next to the door for an easy exit. No long tearful goodbyes, either. Hugs and kisses are great for your kid. Having him feel your heart ripping from your body as he's walking out the door—not so good. Once the car has driven away, feel free to close the door, throw yourself on the floor, and bawl uncontrollably. It's totally allowed and absolutely necessary. Just as long as your kid isn't around.

Start with Email and Gradually Work Your Way Up the Communication Ladder. If seeing each other is too hard, talking on the phone probably won't be a rip-roaring good time either. Email is a great option. Just remember a few important points:

1. **Keep Communication Brief.** No nostalgia, no digs, no anecdotes. Just say what you have to say and hit Send.

2. **Be Polite.** This is a wonderful opportunity to put your manner words to good use. Remember how easy it is to read negatives into an email. Don't leave your ex to wonder if your message had a sarcastic undertone. Be the good example, be respectful, and even if you're not getting back the same courteous response, in time, you will.

3. **Slowly Sprinkle in the Wit.** Once your email conversations get more comfortable and less forced, bring *small* doses of humor into your communiqués. And be thoughtful about the humor. This is not the time to mock or make your ex the butt of your joke. Self-deprecation will go much further in eventually bridging your friendship. Instead of an "In case you were wondering, I don't need to be reminded fifty times that Junior is coming over this afternoon," try for "Thanks for the reminder text about Junior's drop-off time. If I don't have my calendar smack in front of my face, I don't know what's going on."

4. **Try a Brief Phone Call.** When you're ready to communicate via phone, remember to keep it short, keep it to normal waking hours, and make it once a day. Hearing your ex's voice may be difficult or it may bring you joy— especially if you're harboring hope that one day you may end up together again. Either way, take it slow and follow the rules of emailing. Don't sound too joyous (Whoo hoo, I'm dating again!) or too sullen (I've never felt so lonely). Just do your best to be pleasant. Because pleasant is what you want in turn. Pleasant will one day get you to friends, which will one day get you to your version of one big happy family—with different significant others, of course.

Have an Agreed Upon Signal or Code Word that a Fight is Brewing. It's ridiculous to think tempers or emotions will never escalate when you and your ex are in the same space as your kid. A little disagreement you quickly solve? Awesome. But if a heated battle flares up and you're about to lose all your finger-pointing control, either use an agreed-upon hand signal or a code word to alert your ex that you both need to take a step back and a deep breath and try talking through the issue again. Or try again another day.

"Create guidelines," Morely says. "Agree how you're going to fight. Allow for some type of signal, so if a fight is brewing and inevitable, you can get out of your child's earshot."

If your signal incorporates a little humor (think shooting guns you twirl and place in your air holsters for the hand signal or Bran Muffin for your code word), that will also help reset the scene and maybe even squeak out a smile as opposed to a four-letter word.

Haltzman adds, "An argument takes at least two people, so whenever one ex begins to goad the other into some form of disagreement, the proper response ought to be 'Why don't we go into the other room and we can talk about this more?' It may go without saying, but if you were able to avoid battling and argue in a positive and constructive way, you probably wouldn't be divorced." True dat.

Finally, one last "don't" to shield your kid from the messiness of divorce: Don't fish for information about your ex. If Junior wants to be a reporter when he grows up, good for him. No introducing him to the field because you're jonesing for information about your ex. If you know your ex is up for a promotion and you honestly hope he'll get it because he's talked about it *forever*, wonderful. Ask away. Junior will understand you have good intentions for his other parent and will feel comfortable sharing that information. But if the conversation starts with something like, "So, your dad was out late last night, huh?" and moves into, "Was he with a woman?" followed by, "Was she pretty?" and of course, "Prettier than me, would you say?" you're fishing in very deep waters and need to swim to shore, stat.

Trust me, it truly is better not knowing. And if you really, really, *really*, have to know—ask your ex, not your kid.

5

It's All About You

$\mathcal{D}$ivorce can get a brain doing funny things. When I was married, I was thrilled to have Noah's dad take our son to the park or play catch with him in the backyard. I loved that bonding time between a boy and his father. I also loved having the house to myself, if just for a few moments, reveling in a little quiet time. Ah. Nice.

Next thing I know, we're living in different residences, and I suddenly want to be the *only* one who takes Noah to the park—my little one's number one favorite friend (and parent). I also couldn't stop worrying that Noah would prefer living with his dad—especially because my ex was still in our house where our son felt most comfortable. Stories of divorced parents who spoiled their kids rotten, to both alleviate pain and get their little ones to like them better, had always caused me to shake my head furiously in disapproval. But there I was, buying big gifts for Noah with no holiday in sight and offering ice cream before lunchtime.

During this early time of separation and divorce, it's easy to put all your time and energy into your kid, because: A) You're lonely, and Junior certainly does fill a void; B) You're feeling guilty as hell and hope good old fashioned quality time will ease your conscience; and C) You really are trying to ensure that your kid likes you better and never asks to go live with his other parent full time. And while there's nothing wrong with wanting to be a supportive, understanding, and of course, totally amazing parent, there's one person in the divorce equation you shouldn't forget to take care of: you.

When you're on an airplane before takeoff, and the flight attendant is gesticulating at all the exits and showing you how to buckle and unbuckle your seatbelt, the moment arrives when you're shown how to use your oxygen mask. *Every single time*, the flight attendant instructs you to put on your mask *first*, before assisting your little one. Why? Because if you don't have an oxygenated brain, you won't be much help to your kid.

The same goes for divorce. If you aren't sleeping, you're experiencing anxiety or depression, and you've begun to smell pungent, you won't be the über parent you think you're supposed to be. And if you stop taking care of yourself and get sick—well, let me assure you, being a single parent with the flu sucks. Bad. (Note: kids LOVE to jump on you when you're spread-eagled across the bed, feverish, and groaning in pain. And there's no longer another parent standing by to whisk said kid far away so you can get your rest.) Therefore it's in your best interest to make sure you're in good physical and mental shape. For everyone's sake.

I'm most definitely *not* an expert in nutrition and exercise (I'm convinced anything made by the Keebler Elves belongs in that big, wholesome section at the bottom of the food pyramid), and I've never screamed "KEEP GOING OR I'LL ROPE YOU TO THIS MACHINE!" in the face of a flushed, out-of-shape person, who is struggling on a steeply inclined treadmill. Therefore, I've enlisted the help of my friend Peter Nielsen, a fitness expert, author, host of the syndicated TV series *Peter's Principles*, and a former Mr. Universe (he's also divorced with kids) for a few pointers on feeling your best when you don't have the energy to do your best.

Diet and Exercise. If you're not motivated to eat right and work out for the sake of your own wellbeing, then for the love of all things good, do it because if you're going to be divorced, you may as well be divorced *and* hot. Eventually going back into the dating world is going to be awkward and quite possibly terrifying. Knowing ahead of time that you still have the power to turn a few heads (even if the heads have gotten a little older than back in the day) is the ego booster you need before you ask for that first phone number or accept that first dinner invitation.

But I digress.

First, know you need both a healthy diet *and* some type of fitness regimen to get the best results. "You can take five steps forward in the gym, but if you're not disciplined at the table, you're going to take ten steps back," says Nielsen. He adds that hiring a personal trainer would be a waste of money without a proper diet because "eating right is about 65 percent of the equation."

Plus, poor nutrition makes you more prone to disease and heart attack.

Okay, then we'd best talk about healthy eating.

There's a good chance you fit into one of these divorce-diet scenarios:

1. The stress of divorce has you eating emotionally, a.k.a wiping out everything sweet, salty, and/or comforting in your pantry.

2. The stress of divorce has you not eating at all, your life too turned upside down to think about food.

3. The stress of divorce has you expecting to come home to a hot meal, but nothing is on the table anymore, so you hit the fast food drive through.

4. The stress of divorce has you just getting by, which includes standing at the sink and eating straight from a box of whatever was in the cupboard.

This is the time to retrain your brain, and get back into daily, healthy habits. Since you may have less time than ever—or you're more frazzled than ever—a few simple shortcuts will set you on the right path to a healthier diet.

Nielsen suggests planning ahead for the week by purchasing four to six chicken breasts—or a combo of chicken and fish, whatever works and is healthy—then preparing them however you like, all at the same time. Place the finished chicken breasts on microwave-safe plates, cover with plastic wrap, and store in the refrigerator. Then, when you come home from work you can heat one in the microwave, add fruit and vegetables, and you have a healthy meal. Or slice a chicken breast and add it to one of those already-prepared bags of salad. Simple, quick, and no serious thinking required.

Speaking of those fruits and vegetables: Pre-cut anything is good. If you're lacking energy thanks to the divorce, possibly a move to a new home, and the whole single-parenting thing, it's way easier to grab a Hershey bar than peel and cut a cucumber. I know it's more expensive, but trust me, already-cut watermelon, carrots, honeydew, celery—you name it—gives you a fighting chance at eating healthy. (And, once again, looking hot.)

This is definitely the time to make friends with the outer aisles of your grocery store. Try ingesting a few things that don't come in a can or don't require a microwave and punching holes in the plastic covering with a fork. (However, the frozen veggies you can steam right in the bag by tossing into the microwave are a fantastic option and perfect for when you're feeling extra weary.) Just remember, it's all about putting away your daily pint of Haagen-Dazs and pulling out those pre-cut (mmm … so much tastier than chocolate) carrots. Are you feeling it yet?

Now, the fact that you made it to the grocery store and didn't hit the checkout lane with a cart of assorted cookies is already a big thumbs up. But you also have to keep the ol' feet moving. There's nothing like a long walk—or if you're feeling wild and crazy, a brisk run—with some head-banging music to help work through your issues. This is a great reason to invest in an iPod. However, if your divorce left you with a hole where the money in your wallet used to be, don't be shy; pull out that big yellow Walkman that's been shelved in the basement, waiting for its rebirth (retro *is* cool right now), clip it to your waistband (or Members Only jacket), and hit the pavement.

Whatever type of exercise you decide, Nielsen says that to feel good about it and get it to stick, you need to consider two important aspects:

1. **Do Something You Like.** If it's not fun, or it doesn't make you feel good, you won't keep it going. You like jumping on a trampoline? Then dammit, jump on the trampoline. You want to pull out those cheerleading moves from 1987? Make it happen. If you like it, that's all that matters.

2. **Think About Where You Want to Work Out.** If you're not feeling emotionally available, do you want to get hit on at the gym? If you're feeling lonely, do you want to go on long walks in the woods by yourself? Decide what makes the most sense for you at this particular time.

In addition to keeping your heart healthy and your bod looking fab, exercise is a mood booster. And when you're navigating the new waters of divorce, enhancing your frame of mind not only benefits you, but also makes it easier to play nice with your ex.

Another fantastic way to boost your spirits—and look good in the process—is yoga.

"Yoga is good for breathing and meditation, core strength, and flexibility," Nielsen explains. "It gives you a chance to get in tune with yourself. It's not jarring. The benefits are endless."

When going through divorce, Nielsen adds, people often stay busy, which may include going out every night and coming home at 2 a.m. because they don't want to be alone. "Yoga teaches you to be by yourself in a quiet way."

Many of the ladies reading this book may already know the benefits of yoga and have taken classes or followed along with a video at home. So this section is something like a public service announcement for you dudes: yoga kicks ass and a lot of men do it.

A few years ago, I lobbied hard for my husband Frank to go to yoga with me. He had way more back problems than anyone of his age should legally be allowed to have, and he had zero flexibility. Needless to say, he fought me. Just flat out refused to try it. Yoga was for girls. I had to listen to this weekly. For a year. Finally (I don't know if it was a full moon that day or what), Frank suddenly agreed to go. Not happily, of course. It was more like dragging a three-year-old water-phobe kid to an all-swimming, all the time summer camp. If Frank had a tail, it certainly would have been lodged between his legs. He even did his best pouty walk from the car to the yoga studio. One hour later, as we're rolling up our mats to leave the class, Frank looks at me all bright-eyed and says, "Can we go again next week?"

Yoga rocks. It makes your pain go away, makes your body lean and flexible, and it really, really clears your mind. That's about the nicest thing you can do for yourself. Try it at home first if you want to feel more confident before attempting a class. You can rent or buy a bazillion yoga DVDs. Or if you have Comcast, a number of yoga videos for all levels are available free through On Demand.

Make an Appointment with a Therapist. This may seem more like a punishment than a reward, but therapy can, in fact, give you license to experience things you haven't let yourself try before.

My friend Janis started seeing a therapist a few months after her husband left, and she stayed with it for a year and a half. Why? Because it did her a lot of mental good.

"My self-esteem was at a low point and he made me see I had a lot to offer," she says of her therapist. "He reassured me I was handling things pretty well and that a lot of concerns with my ex-husband were out of my control."

But the greatest thing the therapist gave her … was a dog. "I wanted to get a dog, but I knew my ex-husband didn't think we should have a dog, and I worried it would add fuel to the fire," she says. "I'd been with my ex-husband since I was 14 years old, so I was used to doing things his way." She says getting the dog was a great day for her. "I know it was a silly little thing, but this was a huge deal for me. The therapist told me I had a right to have a dog. I guess I needed someone to tell me."

Get a Social Life. Many people who get divorced realize that over the course of their marriage, they let go of most of their friendships. Marriage can be a powerful "it's all about you and me" kind of commitment, where you spend so much time with your spouse, or your spouse and kids, or your spouse and his or her family, that no time is left over for lunches with the girls, fishing trips with the guys, or group nights with the neighbors. (Hello? Anyone want to dust off Pictionary and start pouring shots?)

Thank God for Facebook. Hands down, it's the easiest way to reacquaint with old friends. If you've been resisting the whole social networking trend, fear not: it is possible to keep from turning into a habitual poster. You don't have to note every moment of your life for everyone to see. In reality, you don't have to post a darn thing. You can simply set up an account, browse people who went to your high school or college (so easy to do), or search for old friends who rocked at making you laugh. Send a few messages back and forth, and when you feel comfortable, put out an invite for lunch, drinks, or whatever the heck you feel like doing.

If you refuse to contact people via your computer, dust off your phone book and get to dialing. Or try something totally different and join a class. Whether you've always wanted to learn how to cook, take better photos, or line dance, classes get you out every week. You'll meet people who enjoy the same things you do, and you'll learn new skills. Win-win-win. However you decide to accomplish it, the goal is to get out of the house, spend time with fun people, and start smiling again.

Pamper Thyself. You know how it is when you have kids: me-time is practically non-existent. Unless you're in an unfortunate situation where your ex isn't able to share custody of your kid at some level, you're going to find yourself with time on your hands. I implore you, use that time to take care of you. Get a massage, play a round of golf, sit outside and read a book, go to the gym, or stay in the shower for more than five minutes. Whatever your budget, find something that makes you happy. Something that relaxes you. Or something your ex always refused to do. This isn't selfish—it's vital to your health and well-being. You've been through a lot. You deserve a good dose of TLC.

My friend Leslie didn't start pampering herself until after her second divorce. During that marriage, her self-esteem hit rock bottom. In addition to marriage issues, she was dealing with a work injury that left her in need of surgery, which came with six screws in her neck. "I wasn't taking care of myself," she recalls. "I wasn't eating right. But then I started exercising. The break up gave me confidence to do it."

Leslie started working out with a trainer a few times a week and found time to get manicures, pedicures, and regular haircuts. And then she went on a cruise—courtesy of ex number two.

"I went with a group of friends on a cruise to London," she says. "I wanted to give myself a huge present and I wanted my ex-husband to pay for it. I needed to do something for myself. So I asked. He had a lot of guilt. I called it my divorce gift."

If you do have full custody of your kid, look to friends and family members to help out with babysitting so you can get your me-time. Your situation is even tougher, therefore taking care of yourself is more important. Your kid only has you to count on. You need to ensure you have the wherewithal to take on such a big role and not look and feel like you've aged twenty years as a result. So give yourself a break from time to time, 'kay?

Make an Effort with Your Appearance. Speaking of looking like you've aged twenty years, don't let divorce take away your will to primp. Take care of your exterior. Don't wear your pajama bottoms to the store. Do, however, wear deodorant everywhere. Wash your face before you go to bed. Keep up with your hair. *All* you hair. Men: make an effort to shave. Ladies: You, too. Don't start reliving the '60s under your arms and at your nether regions just because you're living on your own. When you're silky smooth (to whatever degree you dare to rock) and all body-buttered up, you feel sexier. More confident. And ladies, don't forget how to apply a little blush and lipstick. It's about making an effort, which also shows you value yourself. Because my friends, the next chapter is about dating again. And if you aren't feeling and acting like you're worthy now while you're on your own, you sure as hell aren't going to be feeling confident while sitting across the table from a hottie whose only question about the dessert menu is whether or not sex is on it.

Love yourself, take care of you, value you. Take a few deep, cleansing breaths. Very nice. Now, about that hottie…

6

The Rules of Dating

*T*he good news: If you want it and you're ready, a plethora of wonderful people are out there waiting to knock your socks off in the romance department. Whether you're looking to date casually, find a new love, or remember what sex feels like, you can have the kind of relationship (or non-relationship) you want.

However, here's the bad news:

You're back in the dating pool again.

And there's worse news:

You have to date as a parent.

I'm not much of a small-talker, so dating had never been a thrill for me. While I enjoyed the butterflies-in-my-stomach moments, the telling-of-my-story part made me weary, especially having to tell it over again every time I went out with someone new. Add a divorce and a kid into that tale, and it's nothing short of a burden to disclose. When was the right time to mention I was divorced? How much about the marriage and breakup should I share right away? How did

I work in the fact that I had a kid with my ex and therefore will have contact with said ex for rest of life? It was easier to stay home with a *Sex and the City* marathon and a box of Fudgesicles. However, I am a hopeless freaking romantic, and really did want what marriage is all about, so dating I did. And you know what?

It was awkward.

Some guys took the divorce/kid news as if every woman they said hello to was, in fact, divorced with a kid. Other guys quietly faded away (not right in front of my eyes or anything supernatural like that). I was fine with the reaction or lack thereof. It was the blasted storytelling. Each time a suitor didn't work out, along came another one, eager to know my story. Dating was bad enough when I only had to discuss myself. But bringing my ex and son into it never felt natural. It was like dropping a bomb, then waiting for it to blow up in my face.

Of course I met Frank—who became my husband three years later —the *one* time I wasn't looking. Because that's just how it works. He didn't mind that I had an ex or a kid. He had neither, so this was uncharted territory for him. And I hadn't experienced a real relationship since the divorce, so it was uncharted territory for me, too.

The Big Meeting. We dated for a few months before I put Frank and Noah in the same room. I had no set rule on timing—it was more about when it felt right for both Frank and me. I wanted to be comfortable with the situation, but I also wanted him to feel ready for this new role. Because by then we already knew we would eventually get married. And that meant Frank had a lot to learn about becoming a stepparent. I didn't want to scare him off by submerging him into the world of parenting too quickly.

Actually, on one of our first outings together—all three of us, that is—Noah was newly potty trained and still at the point where we had to make a mad dash to find the nearest toilet. We were in a store at the mall, and Frank was in line to pay for a purchase when Noah let out the warning call that peeing was imminent. Knowing how little time there was for action, I grabbed Noah's hand and ran in the direction of the closest department store's restroom, leaving Frank in our dust. And of course, as a non-parent, with little babysitting or uncle knowledge to draw from, he had no idea where we might be. I think half of me was worried about getting Noah to the bathroom in time, while the other half worried if Noah had an accident, Frank wouldn't be able to handle it. Not that he'd given any indication that was the case. I was just nervous about how he would react. I thought because he didn't have kids, nor was he jotting potential baby names in his journal, ready to fertilize at a moment's notice, that kid mishaps had the potential to end our relationship. Don't judge. The brain does funny things when one is back in the dating pool.

Never did I feel more uncertain about Frank's future role in my family than the night Noah nearly peed on him. We were at the point in our relationship when Frank stayed over at my house when Noah was there. I was waiting to get a new headboard and railing, so my mattress was on the floor. It was the middle of the night, and I woke suddenly to find Noah in a sleepwalking state, standing by the side of the bed where Frank was sleeping, pajama bottoms at his ankles and in position to pee—right on my boyfriend. I gasped, and in one swift move grabbed Noah and leaped into the bathroom, getting the seat up just in time. Once he was done, I tucked him back into bed, stumbled back into my own, and pulled the covers high, so jacked up there was no chance I'd be falling back to sleep right away. I was certain getting peed on would be one of the more original break-up stories ever.

Turns out Frank was much more resilient than I gave him credit for. Nine years later, Frank and Noah both crack up like idiots when I retell the "Sleepwalker Pees" story.

But to get to that happy ending, I had to date. And so do you.

First Things First: Are You Ready?

Being ready to date is about so much more than flat abs (or, in my case, a partially controlled pooch) and a repertoire of small-talk topics. You have to be mentally ready before you put yourself out there. That doesn't mean getting all pumped up to hit the bar on a Saturday night and chat up the person seated next to you. Being mentally ready means having healed from all the bumps and bruises suffered during your former marriage. Even the deep gashes that at one time seemed too big for a set of stitches and the widest of Band-aids to mend.

"Divorce is a major lifecycle change," says Morely. "You need that chance to heal." Morely advises asking yourself the following questions: Have your worked out all your feelings? Have you looked at not only what went wrong in the last situation, but also the role you played in things going wrong? If you can answer yes to both, then gradually—and cautiously—begin to date again.

You don't have to like dating to do it. You just have to do it and hope you like it enough to keep going.

My friend Leslie started dating before her first divorce was finalized. She ended up in a four-and-a-half-year relationship, which included her new man and his kids moving into her home two years into the relationship.

"It really was one big happy family," she says of her time with this suitor. "My son loved it." When the relationship ended, Leslie helped her son get through it by encouraging him to stay in touch with the kids. "He's still friends with one of the kids today."

However, Leslie says after her second divorce she changed the way she dated and involved suitors in her kids' lives.

"I'm way more private now," she says. "I'm way more picky about when I introduce someone to my sons."

In fact, after her second divorce, while she might have introduced a suitor to her younger son, she never revealed to her kid that she was dating. It took six years after that second divorce for her to fully bring someone into her son's life again. And she's been in a relationship with that someone for the past year.

"Now he gives my son piano lessons and he's integrated my son into his family," she says. "It's been a great experience."

The Right Time to Reveal

Your eyes met across the room and a force took over, pulling you together. Or maybe you finally caved and let your mother set you up with her bridge partner's still single first born. Either way, you've ended up on your first date, have just figured out you're actually having fun, and you wonder if this charming person smiling at you across the table is going to make a beeline for the door (and take out a chair or two along the way) once you reveal you are not only divorced, but also a parent.

When is the right time to tell?

That depends on how you found each other.

The best part about getting set up on a date is the person doing the setting up can (and should) disclose any need-to-know information to both of you. There's no point wasting each other's time, or getting anyone's hopes up, if you're not looking for the same things in life, or if one of you refuses to live with an ex in the picture for the rest of your lives. This also applies to online dating. If you note in your profile that you're divorced with seven kids—all tantrum throwers— and you hook up online with a cutie, that cutie knows the deal and you get to go without "The Big Reveal."

My friend Janis was divorced a year before she was ready to try dating, which was a big step for her considering she had never dated anyone *but* her ex—since she was 14 years old. Those first dates were all set up through friends or family members, so they already knew her story. "There weren't a lot of guys, maybe five, and they all knew what they were getting," she says. "And because they were friends of my sister, or friends of friends, I felt safe."

You may be thinking, "I love my baby and if some hot thing

isn't cool with that, *I* ain't cool with that." However, after going years without having to date and suddenly being thrust back onto the scene, slightly rounder, possibly heart-broken, and with a back that goes out every two weeks, it's amazing how vulnerable you can be. So whatever you can do to leave nothing a surprise, the better for everyone. That doesn't mean to blurt out your marital status and number of kids each time you shake hands at a business meeting, but do get the information out there.

Haltzman offers more simple and straightforward advice: "There is little stigma associated with divorce these days," Haltzman says. "If the subject comes up, you shouldn't hesitate to apprise any potential dating partner of your status as a former married person."

So there.

What to Share with Your Suitor

You mentioned you're divorced, with a few kids in tow. You possibly admitted you experimented a bit in college. These are all fine things to share. What not to share? That your SOB of a lazy, worthless ex's idea of fun is getting ripped and watching Wrestlemania naked in the living room every Friday night, and what a relief that always was for you because it meant a potential change of underwear was on the horizon. Repeat after me: The less I share, the better.

Don't get me wrong; I'm not saying you should never discuss your ex. But I am saying to keep it short and sweet. Just as you don't want the gory details of your New Love's past relationships floating endlessly about in your head, New Love deserves the same respect. That makes it so much easier to focus on the two of you. Think name, rank, and serial number. Get it out there and get on with it.

My friend Janis says she was grateful to never have a boyfriend— including her current husband—who probed for details. "My husband had the overview of what happened. He knows there were some shortcomings, but I've never been critical," she says. "You can say to somebody, 'It was a horrible time for me and I was badly hurt,' but to go into detail—what's the point? I know people are sometimes alcoholics or drug addicts. That's a whole other issue. I'm talking about people who are fairly civil."

Here's another important reason for not airing your ex's dirty laundry to New Love: New Love may one day become New Spouse. And you want New Spouse to like Old Spouse. That's a key factor in becoming one big happy family. New Spouse isn't going to be digging Old Spouse if you make Old Spouse out as a complete jerk. Consider everyone's future happiness and keep the negative comments to yourself.

Setting Limits in a New Relationship

Got a phone? Check. Got a door? Check. Is your suitor allowed to answer either one? Hell no.

This is a fragile time for you and your ex. Regardless of who broke up with whom, when your long-time partner starts dating again, it's just plain weird. Chances are, you haven't hired a sky writer to announce to the world—and your ex—that you are once again back on the dating scene. You may not even be ready for your ex to know this information. You certainly don't want your kid to find out any other way except from you. And your mother? Are you ready for that barrage of questions?

Keep it simple: Your house + your phone = your rules. Kindly explain to your new love your desire for no surprises. You answer your phone, you answer your door, and you would like to do it without background noise. (Hon? I *still* can't find my thong!) If the relationship becomes serious, you will have to make it known to all involved that this other person exists. (Relax, you get to wait until Chapter 7 for that one.)

Sneaking Your Date Out of the House

. At some point, it's probably going to happen: New Love is going to confuse Junior's schedule (or be too horned up to care) and show up at your doorstep late at night, ready to play Horizontal Hokey Pokey. And you want it just as bad. Before your conscience has a chance to work you over enough to double-bolt the door in New Love's face, you sneak in your hottie, tip-toeing your way to the bedroom, careful not to wake your little one from slumber. Yes!

Hey, you've had some rough days; probably more like rough months. You deserve to get your freak on. And while it's certainly more convenient (and less stressful) to do it on a night when your kid is nestled away at your ex's house, well, sometimes life doesn't work out so conveniently. What's important? *Not* letting New Love spend the night. While you may be feeling ready to introduce your kid to his one-day stepparent, the way to do it is not by having said stepparent-to-be stumble into the kitchen, half-naked, while Junior is downing his morning OJ. Feel free to give yourself a little time for a post-coital cuddle—setting an alarm so you two don't drift off—and then kick New Love to the curb. Figuratively speaking, of course. You'll wake up with color in your cheeks, and not because of an embarrassing situation.

Remember, while you don't want to be thinking about your ex during sex, you should think about your ex in regard to your sex life. The less Junior—or anyone for that matter—knows about New Love, or what you do behind closed doors (or on the kitchen counter), the better for post-marriage relations with your ex. Always keep your long-term goal in mind: to one day create your own version of one big happy family. Be considerate of your ex, and you'll be well on your way.

7

When You Find True Love

*Y*ou've done the dating dance, sambaing with slackers, jiving with juveniles, and waltzing with whiners. Somewhere in that mess of footwork, you stumbled upon a smooth one who quickstepped your breath away. And now you can't deny it. You are officially, deeply in love.

Is it time to let the ol' cat out of the bag?

There are a few schools of thought on this matter. Some experts say to wait until you're in an exclusive relationship where discussions of marriage are likely to come up over Cap'n Crunch and coffee. Others say if marriage isn't on your to-do list (ever again), you can have members of the opposite sex—whom you find deliciously luscious—come by when Junior's around. And still others say incorporate the ones you care about into your lives, but keep them in a friend role when your kid is around. I'll let them battle it out.

"If you've reached a point where you're seriously committed to this other person, you've seriously dealt with your own inadequacies and fears, and you know what you want to do next, you can cautiously bring your child into the relationship," Morely says. "Be sure who this person is; do background checks. You need to make sure your child is safe."

Haltzman believes introducing a suitor to your kid depends on your expectations for both yourself and Junior. "You may not be anticipating long-term relationships, or future marriage," says Haltzman. "You may enjoy the company of some other adults, and there may be no reason to keep that person from meeting your children, any more than you'd resist introducing a coworker or an old college classmate. However, the nature of your interactions with the person you're now seeing should not include intense physical touch until you have a clear understanding this is a solid relationship that's likely to continue. If you choose to have a series of dates over the next several years after the breakup, it's certainly less confusing to your child if you provide minimal exposure to public displays of affection."

"I recommend introducing your kids to someone you care about," Wish says. "However, introduce him or her as your friend and limit exposure to your child, so if you do break up, it's only your breakup and not theirs. Err on the side of too little time and not too much."

My friend Janis dated a handful of men before meeting her current husband. But she made sure that handful had minimal exposure to her kids, including no overnights. Ever. "If they came to the house to pick me up for a movie, I would introduce them to my boys, but that was it until we had dated at least a dozen times," she says. "Then I might invite them over for dinner, along with my sister and her husband, or maybe a couple of the neighbors." Even if her kids were staying the night at their dad's house, she refrained from slumber parties—not necessarily refraining from having a little fun with her suitors, mind you—but no spending the night. While a couple of the guys got close enough to take the boys to a hockey game or other activity from time to time, she says it wasn't enough for it to have any kind of an adverse effect on the kids when the relationship ended.

When her current husband came into her life, Janis incorporated him more quickly into the family, because he was new to town, going to school, didn't know anyone, and was broke. In fact, the day they met, she had all three boys with her, and she was wearing no makeup. They started dating two weeks later. She says that was a good sign. And even though he was around a lot, Janis kept it "platonic and appropriate" in front of the kids. They married five years later and have been married for 21 years.

Wish suggests that once you're truly committed to another person, "Then you can increase the exposure, and you can say to your kids, 'I really care about this person and we're going to be spending a lot of time together.' Once you make that statement, expect your kids to possibly act up. Because the stakes have been raised. They might get scared and anxious. However, that's not a bad thing, because it shows you the degree of uncertainty and fear your kids have. And it puts your potential partner in a position to show you how well he or she can handle that negativity."

Break it to Me Gently

As I said in Chapter 6 (and I quote): "Regardless of who broke up with whom, when your long-time partner starts dating again, it's just plain weird." See that? A whole chapter later and that concept still rings true. While your kid may have (unknowingly) met a suitor or two of yours along the way, your ex probably hasn't. A serious relationship means you'll have to fess up.

How do you break it gently (without a goofy expression of joy plastered on your face), and who do you tell first?

While you might be bursting at the seams to share your joy with your kid (you're imagining him throwing his arms about your neck, shrieking with happiness at the idea of a new parental figure in his life, aren't you?), hold on to that slow motion, After-School-Special moment until you've had a brief, non-emotional chat with your ex.

"If your ex hears news of your current dating behaviors from your child, he or she may begin to form wild fantasies about what's going on, even though it may not be closely related to the truth," Haltzman says. "Also, your ex may believe your child is being exposed to behavior in the home that, frankly, neither of you would approve of. Therefore, by letting your ex know first what's going on, you remove the mystery and open up dialogue."

Morely adds that having the decency to keep your ex in the loop—at least where your kid is concerned—shows your respect for Junior's other parent. "If this person is going to be in your child's life, in the house regularly, going places with you and your child, then your ex needs to know," Morely notes. "You want him or her to be aware so there are no surprises. Plus, you're demonstrating that he or she is still important."

My friend Leslie made sure she let both exes know once she was in an exclusive relationship.

"I'm kind of old-school about that," she says. "I think it's important, especially for the kids. Because they're going to start talking about this person. It's none of my exes' business, but we do share the kids."

Is your stomach flipping a bit right about now? This isn't the easiest talk you'll ever have, especially if you like your ex, even a little. Someone's feelings may get hurt. While you can't help wounded feelings, you can help lessen the impact. Keep it short and sweet, don't gush, and by all means, don't patronize.

The Big Introduction. (The Big Bang Theory—while a more fitting title—was already taken. Thanks a lot, Universe.)

I don't have a clear recollection of breaking the news about Frank to my ex, but I vividly remember the first time they met.

The idea of introducing Old Love to New Love wasn't something I had thought through at all. At the time, I hadn't considered how wise it would be to allow my ex to spend time with Frank, so he wouldn't be concerned about the person spending time with our son. All I saw were red-flashing lights bordering a huge sign that read "Awkward!" So while my ex was aware of Frank's presence in my life, he couldn't have picked him out of a police lineup. (Oh, inappropriate comment, indeed.)

One evening while Noah was at his dad's house, Frank and I enjoyed a quick dinner at a little hole-in-the-wall restaurant in the downtown area where both my ex and I had houses. From our seats at a table near the floor-to-ceiling front window, we had a perfect view of my ex walking by with Noah on his shoulders. Of course we all saw each other at once. Of course they, too, were heading into the same restaurant for dinner. And of course Noah was super excited we were all there at the same time, suggesting we all sit at the same table.

In a situation such as this, you can only grin and bear it. And talk your way around the table-sharing idea. Luckily we were finishing our meal, and also luckily, at a table for two. I convinced Noah to sit at the table next to us, taking the chair closest to me, so we could chat before Frank and I had to take off.

By this time, Frank and Noah had spent plenty of time together. And Frank and I were exclusive, knowing that one day we'd get married, so it was certainly time Frank and my ex got to know each other. Besides, Noah had a perfectly good dad he was with regularly, and since he wasn't looking to Frank as a new father figure, I wasn't overly worried about jealousy issues or territory troubles. I had no reason not to introduce Frank and my ex. It had simply never occurred to me.

In hindsight, I wish we'd planned the meeting, and everyone had time to process and prepare for it. In the midst of the run-in, every emotion I could have at one time was shooting through my body like a pinball. And there I stood, game face on, trying to pretend this was a perfectly normal situation on a perfectly normal day.

Not.

Therefore, before the situation finds you, make time for the situation. Make the introductions. Get it over with. Then pour yourself a nice vodka tonic. You deserve it.

How Do I Live Without You?

You've been living on your own now for awhile, or at least as long as awhile equates to in your brain. Maybe that's six months; maybe that's six years. Either way, it probably took a certain amount of time for you to become accustomed to sleeping across the entire bed and not being able to blame someone else for the hair in the shower drain.

And yet, you're in deep love and thinking marriage—or at least long-term commitment. Should you live together? And if so, where should you live?

Before you can tackle these questions, Wish says, "You have to ask yourself, why are we living together? What are we hoping to accomplish? Usually when people move in together, they're testing the waters. So the question is: can you test those waters without necessarily moving in together?"

Her concern is not about what you can handle, but about what your kid can handle. "Living together is often difficult for kids," Wish notes. "They don't know how much of their heart they should open up. They don't know what role this new person plays in the family. Should they care? Is this person someone who's going to leave? So you want to find a way to learn more about this person as a life partner, while protecting your child."

She suggests developing a more "real" picture of New Love— which includes what this person will be like interacting with your kid—by making the time spent with your potential partner as close to real life as possible.

"Hang out, run errands, go grocery shopping, put Band-aids on the kids," Wish says. "Watch dumb shows on television—whatever it is you do, make your time as real and close as possible to your existing life."

My friend Leslie is still living on her own with her youngest son, but says it's possible her new love could move in. And she isn't ruling out marriage.

"When we first got together, we both talked about never wanting to get married," she says. "But I also want to be that old couple, holding hands. I have this feeling I may want to get married again."

Frank and I moved in together after about a year of being in an exclusive relationship with plans to marry. I agreed to Noah and I living at Frank's house for two reasons: 1) He had a cozy house with three bedrooms and a nice backyard, while Noah and I were living in a two-bedroom rented flat; and 2) It wasn't much of a displacement for Noah, since I wasn't moving him from the home he always knew for a strange place. He had spent plenty of time at Frank's house. We even had his fourth birthday party there in the backyard. So it was familiar. Probably way more likeable for him than the flat. So the move was easy, which was a huge blessing.

However, something that easy-breezy is generally not the case in life, so that means you should consider a few points before deciding the living-together scenario and the location for that next chapter in your lives:

The Family Home, Part Deux. If you're currently nesting in the home where Junior has always lived, you're settled there, and it's a comfortable situation for New Love to move into, that would be the easiest way to transition. Your kid doesn't feel displaced and he still has his neighbor friends and school district to keep him grounded.

This may be as easy as hitting the local mattress store for a new bed and fresh sheets, because, seriously, who wants to claim the love slab where you used to nookie it up with your ex?

While this may not be the greatest of choices for your ex—the idea of another person taking over the house the two of you once fashioned lovingly into a home can be unsettling—it's also easy to explain why this is the best choice for your kid. Keep your reasoning focused on Junior, and you'll get less resistance from your ex.

New Love, New Home, New Adventure. If you're in a transitional home that doesn't have any sentimental value to you or your kid, and is too small for a another inhabitant, consider finding new digs where you can all begin this new chapter together. Make it an adventure, with you, New Love, and Junior all hunting for that perfect abode as a team. Let your kid get excited about selecting his new room or where the TV might go for optimal cartoon viewing. Getting to take a little ownership of the quest will make moving into that new home much easier for Junior.

The best move you can make when finding a new place to live is to keep it within your kid's school district. Whether the idea of a new place to live is exciting or terrifying, not having to start over in a new school, try out for new teams, or find his way through a new group of friends will obviously make for a smoother transition.

However, Wish advises focusing the move on the best school district, even if it isn't Junior's current school district.

"Pick the best school district for your kids," Wish says. "If your kids are doing well and you like the [current] school district, then stay there. If there's a better one and you think it might help, use the school district as your guide. While it's good to keep something solid and the same for your kids, it's not a hard and fast rule. You have to know your children's needs."

New Love's Place is the Place to Be. You may have much better reasons for wanting to move into New Love's place. Maybe that's the person who has the mortgage, and we all know selling a house isn't what it used to be. Perhaps you don't want to start over again in the house where your marriage ended. Maybe New Love has a maid, cook, and butler and why mess with that setup?

While this may be the most difficult transition for your kid (unless the maid, cook, and butler scenario is for real), you can make the process easier by having Junior spend a significant amount of time there before the move, making him more comfortable with the change. This is a good time to let him pick his room, if that's an option, and plan for what he wants that room to be. Paint it his favorite color, frame him a slew of rock-band posters—whatever it takes to make it his personal sanctuary.

If this house isn't in his school district, consider the route my ex and I took. Since we had joint custody and my ex was still living in Noah's school district, we made his house Noah's permanent residence, and therefore our son was able to continue going to the same school. This isn't the most convenient scenario for Frank and me, since that means getting Noah to and from a school that's a good fifteen minutes away (in non-crazy traffic), but it's worth the effort not to completely upend my kid's life.

If staying in the same school district isn't an option, well, Junior will have to work through that. (Unless you're lucky and he isn't all that fond of said school district.) If you can, make the move at the end of one school year, so he has the summer to meet kids in his new neighborhood. Hopefully, New Love has friends with kids nearby, and you can put them all together with a carefully constructed backyard barbeque. Even if you don't know the neighbors well, if you notice they have kids around the same age as yours, make an effort to introduce yourself and Junior to them. If he walks into that new school with one friend he can count on, it won't be such a scary first day.

8

Keep Your Jealousy To Yourself

*Y*ou've made it out into the dating world again. Possibly you found someone who not only makes your stomach flop out of control, but who will also watch the cheesiest of reality shows with you *without* making fun of your guilty pleasure. A special someone who gets along well with your kid.

Somewhere, on another block, in another home, the exact same thing (or close enough) may be going on with your ex. Whether you like it or not.

As I noted previously, I was the one who left the marriage. This was my decision, it was a well-thought-out decision, and never at any point along the way did I regret my decision. Because it was the right decision for me.

And yet, when my ex mentioned nonchalantly over the phone one day that he and some woman I'd never heard of would be doing something together with Noah, a little electric current zipped through my body, ending with a realization that, in my head, it sounded something like "Huh." Because, while I had known first hand of the concept in the workplace, I had never experienced it in marriage (or, I should say, post-marriage): I was replaceable.

"It's often extremely difficult to find out your ex is in a relationship," Haltzman says. "In some cases, this person is no longer with you because he or she decided you're unable to meet his or her needs. Thus, when your significant other finds another person, you can't help but wonder, 'What does this person have that I don't have?' Alternatively, if you found your spouse too difficult to live with, seeing him or her with another person, being attentive, interested, and interesting, can stir up feelings in you of, 'Why can my ex be that way for this other person, but couldn't act this way for me?'"

"I don't think too many people get married with the understanding they're going to get divorced," Wish says. "You want it to work. Even if you have doubts, you still want it to work. So seeing your ex getting cozy and forming a new life and perhaps moving on before you do, or perhaps in a way you wish you and your new partner would, makes things difficult."

Haltzman adds that you may also view this new person as getting to live out a dream you once had for your ex and yourself. Not the most fun thought to have.

And to top it off, your kid is being introduced to a new mommy or daddy figure. Fabulous.

It's sucky enough to break this news to your ex, knowing hurt feelings may occur as your ex watches you putting the pieces back together in your life. Especially when it includes finding someone new to spend time with that your kid may end up really liking as well.

It's so much worse when it happens to you—especially the part about your kid liking the new person.

That Darn New Person. Haltzman says one common reason introducing a new person into the life of the ex is unsettling is because this new person becomes part of your kid's family—without your approval. "If you think about how difficult it was to decide who was permitted to babysit your children, to whom you should leave your children's care to in your will, who should be the Godparents— all those thoughts and struggles went into deciding who would the best possible guardian for your child. Now your decision-making is taken out of the equation," Haltzman explains.

The first impulse is to judge.

"You want to so badly, don't you?" Wish admits. "You want to put them in the NO pile." She advises staying away from using search engines to check out the new significant other, which just gives you more to think (read: obsess) about.

The second impulse is to devour a pint of ice cream, because you feel out of control. You haven't met the person, you don't know much of anything about the person, and you have no idea how your kid is going to react to the person.

"Kids aren't able to make abstractions about character as adults are," Wish says. "This one's fun. This one bakes cookies. This one goes sailing. Some kids are easily seduced with toys, trips, clothes, or money."

I didn't want to think for one minute anyone had the ability to walk into my ex's home and create some type of bond with my kid. Ever. No matter that Noah already liked Frank a great deal and had great interactions with him, already starting to build great memories. Our new family was great. Great, great, great. But only *we* got to be that great, right?

Wrong.

At this early stage in your ex's love game, you can't judge. Yet. Unless you truly do have a solid, serious reason. (Which excludes hair color, better body, or better body. Wait, did I already mention better body?) You can't even bring age into judgment—unless New Person can't yet legally drink, of course—so you're going to have to keep your opinions to yourself.

Now, if needed, there's nothing wrong with a little judging from the privacy of your own home. With Junior out of earshot, that is. Judging from a bar with a good friend is also fair game. Because, let's face it, sometimes you need to fluff out your feathers a bit before you can move on and face reality.

Take an evening or two and a nice glass (bottle) of pinot grigio, and be catty. We can't be mature and civilized *all* the time. Wax poetic—or buzzed—about all the things you don't like about this new person, even if they're the dumbest, most nonsensical issues with no bearing whatsoever on you or your kid's life. As long as your friend is a trusted confidante and is not also friends with your ex—or the new person, for that matter—then you have a good friend with whom to share your emotions, insecurities, and fears. And that's the only type of person who should hear any of this messy stuff.

Keep Your Eyes On the Prize. At this point I want to remind you that the object of this book, and hopefully an important part of your life, is to create your own new version of one big happy family with your ex. That includes your significant other *and* your ex's significant other. Even if your ex doesn't like the idea of you dating again, you can't behave the same way. You're the one reading this book, which means you're taking on the task of being the mender, extending that olive branch, and being the bigger person, so you can forge a friendly relationship with your ex. So you can attend soccer games together and not have to sit at opposite ends of the field. So that one day, when your kid is getting married, he won't have an anxiety attack wondering which of you will be the first to make a spectacle of yourself during the reception. No matter how much you want to criticize your ex's choice in a potential mate, unless there's a real reason that could somehow harm your kid, you can't say a word. Or give that look. Or roll your eyes. Or shrug your shoulders. Or shake your head. I know. I'm taking away all your fun. But it's all for the greater good.

"The important thing to do is develop a sense of observing yourself," Wish says, "and know the situations that can trigger you. If Dad and his new girlfriend drop Junior off at the house and she gets out of the car in the shortest shorts you've ever seen, you know that's going to be a trigger situation. Know that ahead of time. Know what your default behavior is, so you can develop that little voice that says this is trouble; watch your behavior."

See that? Hearing voices—not always a bad thing.

9
Wedding Bells are Ringing Again

*A*h, you and New Love have decided to get married! Congratulations! It's been a long, emotional journey since your divorce and you deserve a wonderful mate who loves both you and your kid.

In the midst of all the reveling, you may feel a twinge of anxiety about the wedding. (Better than having anxiety over your future spouse, right? We're cup half full in this camp.) How do you go about planning a second wedding? How big—or small—should it be? Where should it be held? What will you wear? Who do you invite? Is your ex on the guest list?

Here's the good news: You can do whatever the hell you please.

Here's the (not all that) bad news: There's still a wedding to plan. And if you consider yourself the thoughtful type, you'll have other people to take—at least slightly—into consideration.

Step 1—Alert Your Ex and Your Kid. In That Order. Just like when you broke the news to your ex about New Love's place in your life, you'll have to deliver this news flash gently but honestly. Then, share the news with your kid.

"It's difficult for children to see one parent get married to someone other than the other parent," Haltzman says. "It's important to respect that these important life events you're celebrating may be a source of mourning for your child. Many children hold onto the hope that their parents will reunite, and the concrete step of taking another person for a life partner can be a big blow to your child."

Your discussion with Junior will certainly be a bit more complex than before. Because this time, New Love's role in the household will also be on the docket for discussion. If you've been living together, New Love's part may already be understood, whether that's hands-on parenting, a good support person for the household, or even becoming a buddy figure, depending on what's best for your situation.

I would classify Frank as a buddy figure and minor support person. Noah has a great relationship with his dad and sees him as much as he sees me, so he doesn't need another father. Frank's the guy who plays the Wii with Noah, goes to the driving range with him, and watches goofy shows on TV with him. When required, Frank also does a fine version of what I call "backing vocals," which equates to me scolding Noah for something, such as an incomplete homework assignment, and Frank providing the team player callout: "Yeah, Noah. You have to finish your homework." Not the most helpful, but then again, it's good to have that united front. Seriously, if there were a problem with my kid, thanks to the good co-parenting relationship my ex and I have forged, we would handle the issue together. Then we'd fill in our spouses with how we've decided to take care of the situation. Those are our roles. And you should figure out yours—before you tie the knot.

"Usually, when things are good between the exes, the new stepparent serves as the advisor, the sounding board to the parent,"

Wish says. "They don't take a full parenting role. When they do, it's most often due to lack of parenting and participation from the other parent." She says while the two exes should be the clearly identified parents, if a hole exists in one of those spots, often the stepparent rises to fill the role.

Now that you've broken the news and decided upon your roles, it's ·time to start planning that wedding.

Step 2—Decide Your Type of Wedding. While this could be your second (or third, or fourth) wedding, it may be New Love's first. And New Love may want the whole kit and caboodle, including big, fluffy, white dress, church ceremony, and reception for 300 of your closest friends. We are in an "anything goes" time for weddings, so if everyone is on board, feel free to go traditional.

It could be, the first time around, you had a simple wedding. Maybe you went straight to a justice of the peace at your local courthouse. Perhaps you never left the safety of your car, opting for a drive-thru ceremony in Vegas. If so, this could be your chance to have the wedding of your dreams. Once again, if this is what you want, then by all means go for it. Wear whatever color you please. Put a dozen groomsmen in plaid tuxes if that floats your boat. Invite your entire graduating class if you're feeling it. This is *your* wedding.

If you've been through all the hoo-hah, and have no desire to hit replay on the conventional wedding, you're in luck: there are a zillion other ways to get married, and one of them will suit both you and New Love.

Since I went the traditional wedding route with my ex, I was looking to marry Frank in a simple, yet memorable, fashion. And Frank, who isn't a fan of church ceremonies, all-night receptions, and a final bill that rivals a small house, was totally on board for something different.

After multiple discussions and some good, old-fashioned Internet research, we decided to get married in Jamaica. (Put your hands up for Sandals!) Alone. We had a talk with Noah before pulling out the credit card for the deposit, to make sure he was okay with not being part of the wedding. Not surprisingly, my seven-year-old son was totally fine with not having to dress up and participate in a wedding ceremony. I wore a billowy floral dress (trés romantique!) and Frank wore soft khaki shorts and a button-down white embroidered shirt. We were both barefoot. It was awesome.

And, in an effort to involve our family and friends, we did have a reception when we came home. Outdoors. Catered. Relaxed. Enjoyable. We also had our wedding taped, then played it during the reception, so moms and aunts and anyone else who really cared could watch it. (Next best thing to being there.)

My friend Janis and her current husband had a small wedding with a couple of friends while on a short vacation, but since her husband had never been married before and was very social, she agreed to also do a more traditional wedding in a church where he was active.

"I didn't care about a wedding at all, but I think it meant a lot to him," she says. "It wasn't an elaborate wedding, but a nice one his family was able to come to, along with a traditional reception." And while her kids didn't participate in the wedding, they were all there to witness it.

Find the type of wedding that suits you and make it happen: big, tiny, or complete with a clown. Throw something intimate in your own backyard, followed by wine and cheese. Tie the knot on a boat that goes up and down your local river. Have a destination wedding, either alone, or with the people who mean the most to you. Make it right for the both of you, and you won't go wrong.

Step 3—Involve Your Kid. (Or not.) Just because you have a kid doesn't mean you have to involve Junior in your wedding. There are several different scenarios for what your kid wants/needs:

1.   Junior is crazy for stepparent-to-be and wants to celebrate by taking part in the celebration.

2.   Junior is nervous about adding another person into his family, concerned his place in the house will be lessened with the permanent arrival of New Love, and having an important role in the wedding will make him feel both wanted and needed.

3.   Junior is worried about hurting his other parent's feelings by appearing excited about your wedding, and in an effort to remain neutral would prefer to attend but not take part.

4.   Junior is conflicted in general, and it would be easier for him not to participate.

5.   Junior is fine with the wedding but couldn't care less whether or not he's part of it.

Haltzman says, in an age-appropriate fashion, you should consult with your kid to have an understanding of what role he would like to play in your nuptials.

"In most cases, at minimum, your child should be expected to attend," he advises, "but if he wants to sit out and watch, it's important to turn that around and make it a positive thing. In other words say, 'Just knowing you're in the audience, watching this important event will mean so much to me.' Be prepared for your child to change his mind and want to take a more active role as the wedding approaches. Be sure to find ways to be flexible in terms of including him."

Wish adds that sometimes a kid has issues with loyalty, feeling he shouldn't get close to a new person when he already has two parents. And those issues of loyalty are interfering with his desire to take part in your wedding celebration. "Let him know it's okay to have room in your heart for lots of people," Wish suggests. "After all, when parents get married and they have more than one child, there's room in their hearts to love all of them."

One way to lessen the feeling of being singled out or disloyal is to have your kid share a duty—for instance, being the ring bearer—with a cousin.

Have a good heart-to-heart with your kid, if he's old enough to make this kind of decision on his own. Let him know participation is totally up to him and, while you'd love to have him take part, you won't be hurt if he's not feeling it. And if he says no, you have to stay true to your word. No pouting. No digs about it. Nothing.

Step 4—Consider Your Guest List. Do you know why leaving town or making a quick stop at the justice of the peace are such wonderful options for getting remarried? Because determining whether or not you should invite your ex doesn't come into question. I'm of the close-minded opinion that an ex at a wedding—even if that ex was a former girlfriend/boyfriend—is never a good idea. Why? Because, even if you've been divorced for years, the divorce was completely mutual and amicable, and the ex in attendance is in a committed relationship, watching your ex marry someone else is even weirder than knowing your ex is dating someone else. Why allow any unresolved or hurt feelings to be part of your wedding day?

I also believe the primary reason one ex invites the other to the wedding is because it's the perfect "look what you used to have" moment. There you are, all cleaned up and looking your finest, and you're about to pledge your heart to another person—likewise all cleaned up and turned out—who loves you enough to marry you. And admit to it in front of your friends and family. And you get to revel in all that glory. Sure, it can be a real power trip to put your ex in that congregation of witnesses. But, by doing so, are you accomplishing anything that will move your relationship with your ex in a positive direction for the good of your kid? Will this maneuver push your folding travel chairs closer together at the soccer field or wedge them farther apart?

Maybe you're in a position where you feel obligated to invite your ex. Or you believe not extending an invitation will hurt your ex's feelings. Perhaps Junior wants his other parent there, thinking that having the ex at the wedding signals some type of acceptance by that parent, so Junior can be okay with the wedding as well. If you feel unsure, the best bet is to have a talk with your ex. Explain that you're not certain of proper protocol or what's best for this particular situation. Let your ex know you're happy to extend an invitation (only if you truly are), but in no way do you expect attendance out of obligation, nor would you be disappointed if your ex chose not to come. The most compassionate way to have this conversation is via email. This puts your ex less on the spot, making it easier to refuse the invitation—and it eliminates a potentially uncomfortable face-to-face moment. Imagine how difficult it would be for you to camouflage a pained expression as your ex—whom you're not exactly over—inquires about your feelings over attending his or her upcoming nuptials? Kind of sucky, huh?

My friend Janis didn't invite her ex to her wedding, and says she heard after the fact that he was hurt she didn't extend the invitation. "I didn't think he'd be comfortable attending, so I just didn't invite him," she explains.

My ex and I both got remarried without the other present. Neither one of us felt a need to be there, and we each got to have our special day without any worries of the other. We had our weddings without bizarro feelings or uncomfortable moments overshadowing our happiness. In our opinions, that's how a wedding day should be.

Haltzman suggests contacting your ex before sending an invitation to find out what's best—not only for your ex—but for your ex's significant other as well.

Step 5—Plan That Honeymoon! I really, really, *really* recommend you and New Love enjoy a proper honeymoon. Alone. While it's wonderful you've created this blended family, and maybe you're feeling it would be good for all of you to take off on a vacation together to officially celebrate familyhood, seriously, you two are now a married couple and need quality alone time. With swim-up bar. (Never get out of the water if you don't have to.)

Unlike traditional newlyweds, you aren't starting the marriage with only the two of you. You're an instant family. "Just you and me" moments are few and far between. Unlike a typical newly married couple, when you have a home that includes kids, at what point can you realistically shut the drapes and walk around the house together naked? Or, more important, christen every room in your new digs? (Note: if you *are* doing these things with kids in the house, Child Services will be arriving shortly.) I'm sure there are other fun newlywed adventures I should be adding that involve wearing clothes, but none of those come to mind.

My point, however, remains the same. Take time for a little newlywed bliss. And since newlywed bliss doesn't generally emerge from putting Band-Aids on boo-boos and getting the kids to share toys and forgoing said wondrous swim-up bar for a princess movie marathon, one itty-bitty vacation where you can walk hand-in-hand along the beach—or never leave the comfort of your resort-resplendent bed—is in order.

Take advantage of your ex, your mom, even your new in-laws, whoever you most trust with your kid, and whoever will provide suitable hospitality for Junior—even if it's only for a weekend—and get out of town.

If you absolutely insist on bringing at least one kid with you on your honeymoon, then go somewhere with child-care services, such as a kids' club with structured activities available both day and night, or in-room babysitting, so Junior can fall asleep in your hotel room among his favorite stuffed animals. This will give you an evening or two to enjoy a candlelight dinner while gazing lovingly into each other's eyes, or to take a twirl on the dance floor, with suggestive moves optional, but encouraged.

Wish suggests not taking a honeymoon the minute you get married, unless it's the only time the two of you are able to get away.

"I like people to calm down, get over the wedding, go through the thank-you notes, and set up your house," Wish says. "The old idea of a honeymoon was supposed to be the first time a couple had sex together. That was the value of it, as a brief period before reality set it. Well, reality has already set in if you're remarried."

She adds that waiting to go on a honeymoon reduces the pressure of being forced to leave at a particular time when no one might be available to take care of the kids.

10

Blending Your Own Family

You're newly married again—or possibly blissfully unmarried but in a long-term committed relationship under one roof—and everyone is starting to adjust to the new living situation, including the new/modified roles in the household. But what if you're not alone in having baggage? While it certainly is tidier if you are the only one with the ex and kid, life isn't usually that easy.

Bringing a new spouse into the family can be enough of an adjustment, especially if one or both of you have been managing on your own for some time. My friend Janis had been the only adult in her house for fifteen years before she remarried. And her husband had never been married before, nor had he lived with another woman.

"We made a lot of adjustments," she says. "You can't be on your own for all that time and then just give it all up. Even today we still have separate checking accounts." And for a number of years, there was always at least one kid in the house, coming home from college for the summer, living at home while going to school, or moving back in after graduating. "It was a tag team, but they were always busy with their own lives, coming and going," she says.

So, let's cover some of the family-blending scenarios:

Scenario 1: There's No Kid, But There Sure Is An Ex. You've been reading through this book and working hard to build a solid relationship with your ex that's beneficial to everyone. And even if you're only making baby steps, at least they're baby steps in the right direction. This in no way means New Love is having the same luck.

If New Love has an ex, you may be acquiring an outside person who isn't so happy being on the outside. Or at minimum, won't be happy about your role/presence/ability-to-get-booty-whenever-you-want with New Love. And just because there isn't a kid doesn't mean New Love's ex will be 100 percent out of the picture. There's always a chance that New Love's best friend is married to New Love's ex's best friend. (Did you get all that?) Or maybe New Love married a third cousin, and family reunions are big with his clan. While you may not be thrilled to have this ex occasionally make appearances in your life, it's important to remember one crucial thing: because you've got the kid your ex will always be around, and you will have to have regular communication with that person, no matter how easy or difficult that may be. And since your goal is for all of you to be able to attend Junior's events together, New Love will have to interact with your ex. Forever. You've asked a lot of New Love to work with you on this goal and to be accepting of the relationship you're trying to establish with your ex. The least you can do is be polite to (and patient with) New Love's ex.

Of course, if New Love's ex is behaving inappropriately, regularly contacting New Love, injecting spies into your lives, bugging your bedroom (yes, I've watched a few detective shows, why do you ask?), New Love will have to intervene, and if all else fails, file a restraining order and change the locks on the doors. But chances are the worst you'll have to deal with are a few obvious glares across the room at a mutual friend's wedding. That's not so much to bear, considering you've got New Love keeping you warm at night.

Morely says to remember this isn't your problem, it's New Love's problem—unless that problem just doesn't seem to be going away anytime soon.

"Tell your partner you're concerned," she says. "Find out why this person isn't going away. Is your partner giving mixed signals? What should be done differently? Ask your partner to put something in writing to the ex, either through email or certified mail. The two of you need to come up with a time frame to make it go away so you and your kid don't have to deal with it."

Scenario 2: New Love Has a Kid. And Your House Just Got a Little Fuller. When kids converge in a new family, there will most certainly be an adjustment. And if both kids go back and forth between their parents' houses, you can wind up with a scheduling nightmare.

First, let's take on the idea of having kids from two different families getting used to living together. You'll be dealing with everything from pissiness about being moved into a new home to jealousy. Lots and lots of jealousy. There will be jealousy over who gets which room, jealousy over birthday presents, jealousy over you allegedly being nicer to your stepkid, jealousy over you allegedly playing favorites with your own kid. Unless the kids are grown up and out of the house, you'll have to deal with these jealousy issues.

"Bringing two children from different families into one household is always a struggle," Haltzman says. "Each child comes with a special relationship with one of the parents and not the other. This sets up competition between children for the attention of the parent and stepparent, and is likely going to increase the amount of conflict between the two parents."

He also notes that kids don't feel the need to like each other just because their parents like one another. "In the schoolyard, among ten to thirty children, a child is free to pick out the one or two he wishes to be closest with. When stepsiblings move in together they don't have a choice, but often feel they're being forced by their parents to become friends." Haltzman says the most important thing to do in this case is have patience, and reinforce the need to get along with someone, despite having real differences with that person. "There is some irony here, since the reason you divorced your mate was because you weren't able to get along with someone despite real differences—and that was actually a person you chose," Haltzman notes. "So imagine how difficult it is for your children to get along with your new stepchild, and try to empathize with how monumental this demand might be."

Morely adds that if one of the kids is being rebellious and you can't seem to get it under control, you need a "buy-in" from the other biological parent so the kid understands this kind of behavior won't be tolerated by any of you.

"Rebellion usually happens because the child wants things to remain the same," she says. "First, let the child know you love him and give him permission to talk about how he feels. If you don't see results, the two biological parents should get together with the kid to discuss what will and won't be tolerated. And then all three of you should discuss it. Letting him see the three parents are on equal footing usually takes care of it."

Minding Your Own Business (to Some Degree). If you're a stepparent with a stepkid, who spends time with both his parents, you need to be mindful of how much parenting you're actually doing with somebody else's kid. While you want to do your part to make sure he's following the rules of the house, offering too much guidance (i.e., watching over his homework, getting too involved with his social life, making comments about his wardrobe choices)— all without being asked, that is—will likely earn you the "You're not my mother/father" speech.

"You have to limit yourself and choose your battles," Wish says. "Otherwise you're going to be seen as an upsetter. Treat the child warmer than a guest, but not as close as your own child. Think of the child as a lifelong friend with whom you don't want to stand on ceremony."

While she says it's fine to say, "We don't do that here," if the kid throws something at the wall, it's not fine to say, "You're a little overweight. Should you really be having dessert?" Limit your parenting role if you don't have true parenting responsibilities.

Of course, if your opinion is solicited, feel free to give it. Sometimes figuring out your place in your stepkid's life is a delicate dance. He may need you more if he doesn't have the closest relationship with his other parent. In that situation, you need to take on more of a true parent role. Just take it on slowly. As with a cute, skittish little kitten, you have to let your stepkid get used to you before he'll be okay with you picking him up and carrying him around the house like you own him. Or let's go for a more human example and say, before you get involved in his personal hygiene or his crush on his third-grade teacher.

Now, as far as that schedule goes: imagine, if you will, a house with two kids who have different parents. (I'm only giving you two kids in this scenario so you don't go running, screaming—potentially naked—into the street.) Imagine those kids are school age, possibly going to different schools, possibly with different start and end times. Imagine they're both involved in extracurricular activities, be it a sports team, a dance troupe, or a Britney Spears hair-care club. Imagine those activities sometimes occur on the same day at relatively the same time. Imagine both kids have homework to do and friends to see and birthday parties to attend, and neither of them can drive yet. What are two tired, overscheduled adults—who don't wish to deny their kids—to do?

The best they can and no more.

Scheduling multiple kids when they're with you full time and in the same school district is difficult enough. Getting shared-custody kids where they need to be, especially when schedules clash because you didn't neatly set them up to work in tandem in the first place, is a migraine in the making. You simply have to make the best of it for awhile, and do it without being a slave to the kids. That means every so often you may have to say no to a request, or track down another parent to drive Junior to basketball practice so you can ferry your stepkid to interpretive dance class.

Once the school year is over, the best-case scenario is for all the parents to sit down together, go over which kid is getting signed up for what in the fall, determine practice days, game days, meeting days, etc., and figure out which parent is able to get which kid where. This may be the appropriate time to consider adjusting the kids' house schedules a bit to make the lives of all involved easier. Let's start at the beginning: Do the kids get along and enjoy being together? If so, consider changing their schedules so they're at your house on the same days. Are they having some difficulties adjusting and could use time alone without having to share a parent with another kid? Perhaps opposite days or weeks would do the trick. Do they both have practice on Tuesdays and Thursdays and games on Saturdays, and they're not on the same team? These could be good days for the kids to stay at different houses so they're able to get where they need to go. If the relationship is good among all the parents—yet another reason to put into practice what you're reading in this book—the situation will be easier. Period.

If all the parents aren't yet at that place where they can sit down in the same room without mace being drawn, then take it upon yourself to work out a few scheduling tweaks in your own home, and then each of you can speak with (or email) your respective exes about potential schedule changes and driving duties, with the goal of keeping both kids' lives as close to status quo as possible.

Scenario 3: Kids, Kids Everywhere. What To Do With Them All? You've both got kids. There may be two. There may be ten. How do you keep them organized, disciplined, and happy? While this scenario could be a book on its own, there are a few basic tips and tricks that will get the whole family on the right foot to domestic bliss (or domestic it-ain't paradise-but-it's-not-all-that-bad-either).

Make sure they all have weekly chores that are fairly divided and appropriate for their ages. Wish says, each week have them take turns deciding which chores they want to do. Or if you have two jobs that need to be done, such as taking out the garbage and doing dishes, let them take turns picking which they want to do that day.

Enroll each kid in a sport or hobby they enjoy to keep them busy, creative, and energized. If you can't afford to pay for multiple activities, consider a fair way to break up the cost, such as paying for the oldest kids to participate, and you and New Love helping the younger ones work on their passions at home, whether you're acting as their soccer goalie, or overseeing their art projects.

If you have more kids than rooms, find a reasonable way to assign space. Boys in one room, girls in another is typical. Giving older kids their own rooms and partnering the younger one will certainly be appreciated by the bigger kids who probably want more privacy.

When punishments are in order, once again, make sure they are fair, age-appropriate, and you follow through with them. Don't overlook a wrongdoing because you're trying to gain approval from a stepkid, or because you want your own kid to feel special. And don't cut a punishment short for one of the brood, because when you punish the next kid—and keep the punishment intact for the full term—you will get called out for it. And bad feelings will develop.

Finally, give all kids the freedom and encouragement to speak their minds. Make sure they feel they can come to either parent to express an issue, and consider a weekly family meeting where concerns, ideas, and suggestions can be brought to the table for consideration by everyone in the home. Make it a rule that when one kid is speaking, the others have to be quiet and listen, without interruption, eye rolling, or sound effects. Same goes for the parents. (You know you can eye roll with the best of them.)

Wish says a family meeting is a great way to give kids a voice, but to be effective, it should be fun—at least in the beginning. "Do it over dessert. Cake and talk time," Wish says. "Otherwise, if you're just sitting around a table, the kids will be squirming and getting up to go to the bathroom a hundred times."

While in your fantasy world, you may have envisioned two families combining under one roof and what a Brady-Bunch time it would be. But that probably won't be your reality. So have patience. Take your time. Take baby steps. Seize opportunities to make things easier for your household when they arise. If they don't arise, don't sweat it. Eventually they will.

11

Welcoming the New Wife/Husband

*H*ey! Wow! Your ex decided to get married! This revelation could have you high-fiving anyone in site, even the old man across the street who's still sorting out why you stopped his morning of lawn mowing to high-five his fragile palm. If this is your reaction, either because this means no more alimony payments or you're hoping it will impede your ex from flirting with you during kid pickup, then go right ahead and rejoice. For others, the ex getting married isn't exactly good news.

Mental note: When your ex makes the announcement, your response should be "Congratulations," whether or not that's how you feel.

"What you want to say and what you do say are two different things," Wish explains, "because your goal is to keep the environment between you and your ex as easy to navigate as possible for the sake of your child. Instead of saying, 'Well, I hope she doesn't interfere with what you and I have agreed on,' or 'Oh great, does this mean I have to battle two of you now?' Instead say, 'That's great, I'm glad you're happy, and I know we'll parent well together, because I'm sure you chose someone with good values.' You want to keep it positive."

Whether you left your ex or your ex left you, unresolved feelings regarding your split may still be floating in the air. Yes, I'm talking to you. You two shared a long history packed with memories. A new spouse for your ex mars the importance of that history a bit, even if you're happily remarried and well into the next chapter of your life.

If some grieving is in order, by all means grieve. Ship off Junior to Grandma's house for the night and play your favorite high-school mix tape of gloomy break-up songs. You deserve one good night of total shut down. Get it out of your system quick, though, because you and your ex's spouse need to find common—non-threatening—ground for the sake of the kids, and you won't achieve that with puffy eyes and a ratty tissue stuffed up your nose.

Roll Out the Welcome Mat. As the ex, you're the one with the power—whether it feels that way or not. Before you start pondering the contents of my beverage glass (ice water, thank you very much), consider this: You had your ex first. You know your ex best. You share a kid with your ex. You probably helped with picking out and/or purchasing some of the clothing and household items in your ex's abode—which your ex's new spouse is surrounded by. And somewhere deep down, your ex's new spouse wonders, if only every so often, if your ex still has feelings for you. See that? You're practically terrifying to your ex's new spouse. Therefore, it's largely up to you to foster a decent relationship with that person.

The most important things you can do? Be nice. Smile, shake hands, say, "Pleased to meet you." —even if you're not.

The worst things you can do? Behave coldly, give disapproving looks, make a snide comment to your ex's new spouse, make an I-know-you-better-than-this-rebound comment to your ex. Just as bad: trying to become the new spouse's instant best friend. No toothy grins and big hugs when you first meet. No overexcited gasps of joy followed by pleading for wedding details. No becoming Facebook friends. A little distance between households is a good thing.

It's all about baby steps. Just as you would a boss, or a future in-law, take things slow. Start with short bursts of small talk during kid exchange or at a soccer game, and build from there. Don't strive for real friendship. Not to say it doesn't happen sometimes, and you might find that your ex's new spouse is a really cool character who's fun to be around. But think about it: Would you want New Love and your ex out for the evening, talking over beers? Wouldn't you be slightly concerned what's being said about you, or worse, what each one is finding out? Kind of horrifying, right? That's generally how your ex would feel if you tried befriending the new spouse.

I remember my twenty-year high school reunion. I was there with Frank and my ex was there with his wife. (My ex and I were in the same graduating class.) Our new spouses were friendly with some of our classmates and their spouses, and everyone knew my ex and I were on good terms, so it was a nice situation where everyone could chitchat with each other and nothing about it felt unusual. That was, until a couple of hours into the evening, after Frank and my ex—and virtually everyone at the reunion except for me—had put back a few drinks. (I was nine months pregnant, big as a house, and without alcohol.) I began to realize that every time I circled back to Frank, he was beside my ex and they were chatting and laughing like crazy. I would have felt better about the scene if my ex's wife had been part of it, but she was hanging out with a few classmates' wives out of earshot. To this day, I don't know exactly what Frank and my ex were talking about, but at one point I heard my ex remark, with a bit of a slur, "I know. I *was* married to her." And Frank cracked up as if he had completely forgotten that the person he was talking to had once been my spouse. I whisked in and dragged Frank away to the bar for a double Sprite. No ice. That was all the buddy-buddy behavior I could take.

Always remember, combining flames with alcohol is surely going to lead to an explosion.

My friend Leslie willingly rolled out the welcome mat for both of her exes' spouses. And while she has different relationships with each, she's happy to have both of them in her kids' lives.

Regarding ex number two's spouse, she says, "We get along great. I thank my lucky stars for her every day. She's a fabulous stepmom and a wonderful influence on my son." In fact, she says finding out ex number two was getting married was thrilling. "I rejoiced, because I knew he wasn't going to call me anymore. He had someone else to pay attention to, and she's great."

Leslie also says that welcoming ex number two's new wife, her family, and her kids was the key to a better relationship overall with her ex.

Wish says a new spouse can often view the ex-spouse as intimidating, because the new spouse doesn't feel part of the "in crowd." (See that? We are *totally* intimidating.)

"They don't know the kid, they don't know when they have a say, they don't know all the history, and they don't know their role yet," Wish says. "It's hard for a new spouse to find his or her way."

How do you make that introductory period easier for the new spouse? Wish suggests sending a small token. "Notice what color the new spouse wears or what he or she is interested in and get them a little something, even a gift certificate to a favorite store," she says. "Make the effort."

She also advises knowing the new spouse's birthday, as well as names of the various family members. And be flexible.

"There are lots of variations of good people," Wish says. "If your ex's spouse has fifty-two tattoos, that doesn't mean he or she is a bad choice. Get to know that person."

Getting the 411 On The One. Are there things you need to know about your ex's new spouse? Sure. Do those things include clothing size or sex frequency? Uh, no. All you need to know are things that could possibly affect your kid: Previously married? (Need to know if that ex has issues that could become a problem.) Recreational-drug habits? Handgun owner? Kids? Kids with recreational drug habits, who own handguns? Get the facts, get them from your ex—in a non-threatening, non-accusatory way, out of earshot of your ex's new spouse—accept the answers, and don't ask again unless something comes up that makes you question the responses you were given. While you do want to protect your kid, you also need to balance the trust, as long as your ex is overall trustworthy. (Note: if your ex cheated, do *not* use that fact as some kind of trump card, insisting on more detailed information that's clearly not necessary, all in the name of "I can't trust you anymore." Minus the huge screw-up, if your ex had, in fact, been someone you could trust in other aspects of your life together, particularly where your kid was concerned, resist the urge to hold a grudge, which could potentially harm your kid's relationship with his other parent and new stepparent.

Now, of course, if you find out your ex's new spouse has a record for abuse, or some other serious issue, you have legitimate grounds to complain. Otherwise, be careful not to act on rumor or misgivings.

"You don't want to set up your ex to hide things from you or lie to you," Wish says. "If you've heard someone has a hot temper, unless you've seen it or there's evidence of it, you can't do anything about that." Wish advises staying alert. "Check for bruises. Watch your child's behavior. Does he not want to talk about time spent at his other parent's house? Does he change the subject? Is he moping?" If yes, then it's time to speak to your ex about possible trouble.

Turning Small Talk Into Mutual Respect. Your directive with your ex's new spouse should not be to form a great friendship. What you should look to get out of this relationship is a person you can trust—who can also trust you. When you're around each other, you should both feel comfortable and safe, with the ability to carry on a social conversation. Out of that will grow a respect that should help you get through any kid issues that arise in the future.

My ex's new spouse and I did a great job at giving each other the friendly wave during Noah's pickup or drop off. She has always been a kind person, for which I am fortunate, and if I step into their home while waiting for Noah to collect his necessary things for my house, we can chat about work, our parents, and the upcoming school year. These are safe, comfortable subjects, and demonstrate we are truly interested in each other on a basic, but thoughtful level.

Not until Noah was around six years old did my ex's new spouse and I find ourselves with alone time. Both our sons were taking the same swimming class at a local gym—a class that took place while my ex had to work. This was one of those classes where it didn't make sense to leave and come back—plus I'm a paranoid mom and prefer watching over my young kid while he's swimming laps—so we found ourselves with a good hour to kill once a week for six weeks, sitting side by side.

As I noted earlier in this book, I'm not the greatest with small talk. I find it forced and generally uninteresting. When I have to do it, I manage, but when possible I do my best to avoid it. So there I was, sitting beside my ex's new spouse, realizing I couldn't check email on my cell phone for the duration of the class, without looking totally rude, which left me no other option but to begin talking. Know what happened next? I found her easy to chat with and likeable. We couldn't be two more different people, but thanks to that swim class we found we can pass time together in an enjoyable manner. And boy, does that make all the difference in the world.

My friend Janis rolled out the welcome mat in a big way for her ex's girlfriend—with whom he's been living for about twenty years— by inviting them both to her and her husband's home for a variety of occasions, from Christmas to Labor Day pool parties. And the two couples couldn't be more different.

"Part of it is, my ex-husband doesn't have a family other than his partner," she explains. "He doesn't have siblings. His parents are long deceased. I always wanted to make him part of things our children are part of, so that's what started me doing it. And my husband always makes sure we invite them." While she admits her ex and his girlfriend were ill at ease at the beginning, now they're all comfortable with the get-togethers.

Part of that comfort level came from Janis being warm and welcoming, even though she and the girlfriend have nothing in common. "We're very different people, so it's not like we'd become buddies. However I try to make her feel good when she's here."

Welcoming the New Stepsibling. If your ex's new spouse has a kid, and that kid has formed some level of friendship with Junior, it doesn't hurt to include Junior's stepsibling for birthday parties and other appropriate events. Your kindness to the stepsibling will go a long way in nurturing your relationship with both your ex and your ex's new spouse.

Noah's stepbrother is two years his junior, and when we first met he was exceptionally shy around me. That wasn't a surprise—I can't imagine what he thought of me or how he felt having me around his new family at classes, soccer games, and the like. He was a sweet kid who looked up to my kid, and they did seem to enjoy playing video games together, so I invited him to Noah's birthday party. This turned out to be a good experience for everyone. He got to be at our house for a fun reason, the boys were able to hang out together, and my ex and his wife had a bit of alone time for the duration of the party. He even took a shine to Frank, as most kids do, and had fun shooting hoops with him, along with the other kids.

Since then, he's had sleepovers at our house a number of times, sometimes because we invited him, and sometimes at my ex's request so he and his wife could attend a function. If we can oblige, we do. That's why the one big happy family scenario works. We all try to be good to each other, even if it's a little inconvenient or different from the original plan. If your current state of divorce has you thinking you'll never reach this level in the relationship, all I can say is, in the beginning, neither did I.

12

Incorporating a Stepparent

Sometimes it's difficult trying to parent with your mate. One of you may be too lenient or too strict. One of you may get a little lazy about seeing a punishment all the way through. One of you may continuously be late picking up Junior from school or getting him to practice on time. Finding common ground and learning how to overlook things can practically be an art form.

So imagine trying to parent with your ex-mate, while incorporating your new mate and your ex's new mate into the mix. (Can anyone say in-home bartender?)

It seems as if, just when you finally worked through the struggles of consistent parenting with your ex—or at least something that resembles a united front—along comes a new person crowned with the "parent" title, and the next thing you know, your kid has three, maybe even four authority figures telling him what to do. Who does he listen to and how does he distinguish who has precedence?

And if you think it's hard enough for your kid to deal with

someone who isn't his actual parent getting involved with his life, this can be even more difficult for a parent to handle.

To be honest, there was a moment when I almost blew up at my ex's new spouse. She didn't do anything terrible by any means. What she did do was get a little too involved in the parenting of my kid. In hindsight, I can see she was rightly frustrated with Noah and only trying to help. However, in the moment, when another person—no matter who it is—tries to assume your parenting role, emotions tend to escalate.

Wish says in a situation like this, "Talk to your ex; don't confront the stepparent. And make it positive. Say, 'I understand Junior was sent to bed without dinner. You and I haven't talked about that yet. Is that a new technique you're working on?' You want to make it easy for your ex to explain. Then say, 'What can we do in the future?' Make it as easy as possible for your ex to tell you what's going on and keep a dialogue going with you."

I had gotten so worked up over this incident that I requested a meeting at a coffee shop with my ex. This was something we'd never done before. If there was an issue, we discussed it via phone or email. But my emotions were all over the place, and I needed a face-to-face conference. In a public place. Mostly so I wouldn't yell. Or start crying.

Let me take a moment to say that, in addition to not enjoying small talk, I hate confrontation. Despise it. And I've always tried to be good to my ex, because not only is that who I am, but that was also part of the grand plan of our one big happy family. But having another party get involved with my kid took me emotionally to a place I hadn't known before. We were in uncharted territory for the first time in a long time, and we needed to establish new rules.

We had an uncomfortable talk. I was honest about my feelings. We came to an understanding that, when it came to parenting our kid, we were the parents and our spouses played supporting roles. If there was a problem it was up to the two of us to handle it. Period.

Of course, this will be different if you and New Love have sole custody of a kid, be it your own or New Love's kid. Then you both have to assume true parenting roles. Otherwise, steer clear of getting too involved in the disciplining of someone else's kid. Just as you don't want other people parenting Junior, they don't want you parenting their kids either.

Giving a Stepparent the Green Light to Intervene. Is there ever a time a stepparent should step in? Absolutely. In times of imminent danger, by all means throw your weight around, put your foot down—whatever body part is needed to stop the looming doom, use it. What classifies as imminent danger? First, breaking a household safety rule, such as driving in a car without a fastened seatbelt, riding a bike without a helmet, or riding a bike, texting, and crossing a busy street at the same time. Second, doing something illegal: drug use, sneaking a beer, shoplifting. Finally, anything that's just wrong: bullying, harming another person, sexting. Any of these situations need to be broken up immediately, no matter by whom. However, the aftereffects of the situation, including the well-deserved lecture and the whale of a punishment, are something that should be dealt with later. By the parents. And hopefully, they'll remember to thank you for caring.

Authority Versus Parent. It's important to have a sit-down with Junior—preferably with all parental figures included (otherwise have your own meeting and ask your ex to do the same) to discuss the stepparents' role, so everyone is clear on the parents' wishes. If you have a situation similar to mine, where both parents are actively involved with the kid, with stepparents taking on that supporting role, it's important for the kid to understand that, just because the stepparent may not dole out punishments or make life-changing decisions for him, this person is still an authority figure who deserves respect. If the kid is watching TV and the stepparent asks him to take a break and set the table for dinner, the kid should get on it. Not blow it off. Not cry, "You're not my parent!" Not explain that he'll be waiting to receive the directive from his "real" parent. These are simple, daily moments that require someone to be in charge, and just as that very kid would do exactly what his teacher or coach tells him to do—not actual parents but definitely authority figures—so should he do what the stepparent asks.

"First sit down and go over parenting roles with your ex and make sure you're on the same page," Wish says. "Then explain those roles to your kid." She suggests working it along the lines of, "Mom and your stepdad are going to work like a team to care for you."

My friend Leslie says her exes' spouses are seen as more of an aunt than of a parent.

"We, the parents, are responsible for the actual parenting and punishing," she says. "It's great because they don't get the 'You're not my parent' repercussions from the kids. Unless there is danger, all punishments come from the parents."

When an Issue is Yours and Yours Alone. Not every problem with your kid should be a group effort. For instance, any issue dealing with hurt feelings (i.e., a broken heart, a major disappointment, or a backstabbing) does not need to be brought up at the table during a family dinner with New Love and the stepsibling on hand to provide unwanted commentary. Sometimes Junior needs a private moment with just you, or perhaps both his parents, and wishes his issue to remain just that—private. Hear this: it's okay not to tell New Love every detail about your kid's life. You can share with New Love that your kid is having a problem, say, with school, that he asked you not to broadcast. This way, New Love knows something's up that could affect Junior's behavior, but you haven't broken your kid's trust.

Reviewing and Refining Roles. Does everything always work out as you intended? Of course not! You're reading this book, aren't you? Therefore, what you'd like to have happen with your new family and what actually happens may be two different things. Perhaps you're working more than you'd like, and New Love is playing a more active parenting role during your absence, therefore requiring greater authority than originally planned. Maybe New Love has a kid living with you too, and when the stepsiblings get in trouble together, it's difficult to punish one kid (grounded, no electronics) while the other waits for you to get home to discuss (and he's enjoying his favorite shows while he waits).

There are a plethora of reasons why the original rules aren't working. Don't distress. Talk to New Love. Talk to your ex. And don't forget to talk to the kids. Come up with a new plan and give it a go. A little trial and error is commonplace when mixing families and each person's emotions, history, issues, fears, and frustrations. Keep those clichéd lines of communication open. Don't be thickheaded. Be prepared for bumps in the road. Eventually you'll have smooth sailing.

13
Keeping Your Distance

*Y*ou may have been married one year or twenty-four. No matter the length, the time spent together comes with an intimate knowledge on everything concerning the other person, from skin care regiments and snoring after Thai food to latte preferences and (not so) secretly recording all the *Real Housewives* to watch when insomnia strikes. You know your ex. And your ex knows you.

Repeat after me: This knowledge is *not* something to flaunt in front of your ex's new spouse.

It can so easily slip out, too. Picture the scene. You're at Junior's soccer game and it's a big moment. You're sitting with your ex and the new spouse. Potentially a few other family members are present as well. Everything is going fine. Junior passes the ball to another teammate without having it stolen away, and you all clap, nod enthusiastically, and exclaim to one another how much he's improving. It's pleasant. Practically fun. Then your ex's new spouse leans over to your ex and mentions something about a movie they're planning to see that evening. And you chime in with, "Remember that time we went to see *Gigli...*" and you're off and running, animatedly retelling this funny, memorable moment you and your ex experienced together while you were still married to each other. One of two things will happen next: your ex will either shrug off your story in an attempt to not alienate the new spouse, leaving you feeling stupid and inappropriate, or your ex will indeed remember just how hilarious that moment was and join in on the telling of the story, creating for the new spouse a nice image of the two of you as a happily married couple.

Either way, the mood at the soccer game will immediately change. Someone will have hurt feelings, and that someone may hold onto those hurt feelings, potentially damaging a relationship you've worked hard to foster. The vision of one big happy family just got a little hazy. Yes, because you reminisced.

Reminiscing, no matter how innocent, is dangerous territory. You may have no intention of being a threat, but a threat is what you become. Because reminiscing plants an image of something that once was—a picture your ex's new spouse can never erase, no matter how bad your marriage might have been or how spectacular your ex's new marriage may be. And even though it's natural to be reminded of a moment and share your thoughts, you must resist. Even if it's killing you, this is all for the greater good. If you cannot go without the retelling of the story, call your friend. Call your second cousin. Call anyone who enjoys a good story. Just don't call your ex. Or your ex's new spouse. Or any of their family members. You get my drift.

For the sake of your ex (who may still have feelings for you), your ex's new spouse (who may be unsure of you), and your ex's new stepkids (who may lose any feeling of stability around you), be conscientious of how you interact with your ex.

"Put those boundaries in there," Wish advises. "It's okay to feel like you're friends, but there shouldn't be hugging goodbye or anything. It's too confusing for the kids and it could ignite World War III with the new spouse."

Morely notes that even though there should be boundaries, you should continue to be yourself in these situations—maybe not right at the beginning of a split, but once things have calmed down a bit.

"As long as everyone is strong enough, you should be able to tease. You shouldn't have to walk on egg shells," she explains. "Don't be too tentative. If you're a joking person, you should be able to do that. You're trying to show your children how to get along. You're modeling for them."

What Else Not To Do Where Your Ex Is Concerned

1. **Give "The Look".** Most people have a look—that I-can-see-into-your-soul stare. It's familiar. It's intense. And also obvious. For that matter, control all the items located on your face. Don't bat the eyelashes, don't pout the lips, don't lower the chin a tad and look out knowingly over your glasses. I'm not saying don't make eye contact with your ex, but let that eye contact be the same you'd give the old, slow, check-out lady at the grocery store. You wouldn't flash her a come-hither glance, now would you?

2. **Be Touchy-Feely.** I admit it. I'm a hugger. We have one drink together—I'll give you a hug. We fall into a brief conversation at an event—you're getting a hug. I hug everybody. But I don't hug my ex. Why not, you ask? *Why would I?* Hugging can be harmful. Whether you were left or did the leaving, if you give a hug, it can either make your ex uncomfortable or provide a surge of electricity. Either way, it's going to harm the relationship you're trying to repair (and keep platonic, thank you very much).

Besides, do you honestly think your ex's new spouse would be happy about you hugging your ex? Or touching your ex in any familiar way, be it a hand on a shoulder or a playful swipe? Maybe in a dozen years from now, when Junior's getting married, everyone has *really* moved on, and it's become difficult to remember ever being together, you and your ex can share a hug and congratulate each other on bringing up a great kid. Until then, restrain.

3. **Grant Your Ex Too Much Attention.** You're at a wedding for a mutual friend—a friend who decided to put you, New Love, your ex, and your ex's new spouse at the same table. (Obviously not that good a friend.) You and your ex, having shared a friendship with the person for many years, obviously could talk all night long about said buddy, along with all the other people in attendance whom you also both know (and have stories about). While a funny tale or two, told by one of you (without the other interjecting dialogue, which turns into a rousing bit of back and forth) that does not include bringing up you and your ex as a couple in order to tell the story is acceptable. Then turn to the person who accompanied you to the wedding, and give *that* person your attention for the rest of the evening.

Treat your ex as you would a likable acquaintance. You share a pleasant exchange, you maintain good feelings with each other, and that's pretty much it. That doesn't mean you can't talk to each other for the rest of the night—a comment about the drunk guy by the bar, hitting on the girl young enough to be his daughter, can be shared with your entire table, your ex included. Just don't direct your commentary only to your ex. Don't whisper either. Please.

4. **Stay Too Chummy With Your Ex's Family.** Let me share a story about my friend whose ex and family refused to divorce, even though she legally was. Her ex and her family were so friendly that she would show up to family events—weddings, picnics, Christmases—and he'd be there. And she wouldn't even get a heads up! She would breeze in, arms filled with presents, feeling joyful, and suddenly, she stood face-to-face with her ex. And her day would be shot, because their marriage ended badly. *Badly.* And they had no kids. Bad marriage. Bad divorce. No kids. While she repeatedly asked her family not to invite her ex to events she was also attending, they refused because they *liked him.* That's a good reason to piss off a person who shares your blood. Over time, my friend felt so angry and

hurt by her family's lack of sensitivity, she was ready to divorce them as well. This is why refusing to respect the wishes of a person who has gone through a divorce comes with deep repercussions. So does maintaining besties status with a family you're no longer related to.

When my ex and I were married, my mother-in-law was one of my best friends. We saw each other a good three days a week, taking yoga classes, going to estate sales, or just getting together with the family. I adored her. When I left my marriage, needless to say, my ex wasn't the only one I hurt. However, having had such an affinity for one another, and considering the great post-divorce relationship my ex and I forged together, it was only a matter of time before my now ex-mother-in-law and I were sitting next to each other again at soccer games, chatting about movies and book picks.

However.

Just because we have a friendly relationship doesn't mean that I try to behave like her daughter-in-law or her best friend. She has a new daughter-in-law, and she likes her very much. If I were to vie for my ex-mother-in-law's attention, it would only add a layer of discomfort to what has been a perfectly lovely situation. It's great that we can chat at an event, or that she can call me about Noah spending the night at her house. That's how it should be. But I shouldn't be calling her for dinner. Or to gossip. Or to go bowling. I have my own family and she has hers. I will always adore her. But if I want to make this relationship with my ex and his family work, I have to respect boundaries, no matter how much I wish I didn't have to. Sometimes you have to make sacrifices for the greater good. For me, this is one of them.

5. **Use Your Ex's Friends.** When you get divorced, usually one of three things happen where your mutual friends are concerned: they maintain separate friendships with you and your ex; if it's a couple, the woman stays friends with the woman and the man stays friends with the man (and then they report back to each other, of course); or

they take sides, severing ties with one of you as if you'd never been more than a casual acquaintance.

If you do maintain a relationship with a mutual friend, make sure your only motivation for staying friends is because you *like* that person. Friendships are such an easy way to keep tabs on your ex. It only takes a couple of beers with a mutual friend to make a teeny-tiny comment about your ex seem like a natural transition of topics.

"So, I hear Roger is looking for a new job. What does the wifey think about that?"

"Linda's looking a little bigger these days. She blimped out right after we got married, too."

And then off you go, gathering information for the next hour on all things ex.

How do you know that very friend won't be reporting this conversation back to your ex and/or your ex's new spouse? Or reporting to another friend, who happens to mention it to the very people you've been prattling on about? Let's face it: just as you gossiped, so does most everyone else. Loose lips not only sink ships, they can seriously screw up your mission to build a solid relationship with your ex. If you need to talk about your ex or your ex's new spouse, do it with a friend who doesn't know them. If you're maintaining friendships with people for the sake of keeping your finger on the pulse of your ex's new life or in hopes of keeping your ex abreast of you, divorce them too—and quick.

14
Considering Another Kid

$\mathcal{H}$umans are funny. Just when we get our lives under control, we always manage to throw something new into the mix, just to keep it interesting. (Or just to see how much we can bear.)

Like another kid.

While it's natural to want to fornicate with New Love, alas it's also natural to think about creating a new kid together. But are you ready for it?

Wish suggests waiting until you've been married at least two years. "That's about when the honeymoon period is over and you truly settle in to what life is really like," she says.

Wish also notes that if you already have a little one, it's helpful to wait until that kid is school age, preferably around nine. "The brain goes through several growth spurts maturationally," she explains. "The first, on average, is eight. If you can get to that first hump, you've got a child who can better handle emotions like jealousy, ambivalence, and anger."

When Frank and I first met, I was on the fence about having another baby. Life was busy, Noah was amazing, and Frank had never put having a kid of his own high on his priority list. When the discussion came up as we talked about first moving in together and then getting married, I stuck to the same story: I may at some point want to have another baby.

I required options, not definite answers. For a few years, I wavered back and forth, sometimes thinking how joyous it would be to create an itty-bitty baby with my husband, and other times thinking my life was full and wonderful and wondering what the point would be of messing with that.

And then a funny thing happened. I woke up one day and realized I was nearing forty. If I was going to have a baby, I didn't want to wait another couple of years. I wanted to be able to afford to retire and enjoy my grandkids someday. I also wanted Noah to have a sibling. And, just like that, I was ready to grow our family.

Frank, however, wasn't quite convinced.

As I mentioned, becoming a daddy wasn't something Frank daydreamed about. In fact, he may have had a few nightmares about it. Needless to say, trying to get pregnant was not something that happened early on in our marriage. We waited three years. Something about that particular time in our lives finally felt right for us. Noah was older, we were living in a larger house, our finances were stable, and we were solid in our marriage. And so we decided to jump.

My Baby Didn't Want a Baby. I became pregnant after three months. And even though initially, Frank was on the verge of fainting every few minutes once he got the news, it was Noah who experienced the greatest trepidation.

Many moments of my life have become a bit hazy over the years, but sharing my pregnancy news with my son, I'll always clearly remember. Having adapted so well to all the other changes that came his way over the years, I assumed adding another person to our family would be no big thing. The way his face curled up the instant my news was out told me I should seriously stop assuming things.

He cried and cried and cried. The kid was inconsolable. My joy was quickly capped. My heart broke for Noah. I didn't know how to make it better for him. After the tears had streamed down his cheeks for some time, I finally got up the nerve to ask him why the idea of a new baby was so upsetting to him. Noah blurted out, "Brothers are so annoying!" After more questions, I realized he was talking about his stepbrother, who lives full-time at my ex's house. Noah was nine at the time. His stepbrother was seven. He was at the age where he wanted—and sometimes helped himself to—Noah's things. And that's when I realized my kid thought I was going to give birth to a seven-year-old boy, who would forever be in his room, taking all of his favorite possessions.

Once I explained to Noah that he and his new sibling would be ten years apart, and would never be into the same kinds of things at the same time, his entire body relaxed. His face settled into an easy smile. I knew everything was going to be okay.

As important as it is to make sure the baby topic has been thoroughly discussed and agreed upon with New Love, it's equally important to ensure your kid has a good handle on what expanding the family really means.

While some kids look at having another baby as being replaced—whether or not a divorce is involved—your kid may experience a variety of emotions over a new baby.

"Some kids want a same-sex sibling, while others want an opposite-sex sibling," Wish says. "They either want a playmate, or they don't mind letting in another kid, as long as they get to remain the only boy or girl. Then other kids feel, because they're the product of divorce, that they're flawed and whatever child you and your new partner have will be the good one."

Morely suggests preparing your kid before you get pregnant. "It really makes a difference if you prepare him ahead of time," she notes.

"Find out how he feels about it. Let him know he will be loved and will continue to be important in your lives. Make sure the attention is still there. Let him still sit on your lap, take him out to lunch, go to his games. Don't make the child feel excluded."

Preparing for Baby (with Your Kid)

There are a number of ways to include your kid in the baby planning so he feels, well, included.

Name Selection. You don't have to go with his choice of Darth Maul, but having your kid chime in with baby names (that don't get shot down—he's just a kid!) gives Junior a sense of contributing to this big event, and will begin his connection with the baby.

If he's old enough to read, let him browse through a baby-naming book, either highlighting choices he likes or copying them onto a page of the baby's memory book. When he's older, Junior will get a good laugh at his list.

Decorating the Nursery. Preparing a room for Baby is an enjoyable family project because, let's face it, baby stuff is tiny and cute. Let Junior select the color scheme from a few pre-approved palettes. If he's old enough, have him surf the Web for nursery themes, printing out his top three for consideration.

To keep baby shopping interesting for him, allow your kid to pick out one thing for the baby's room that's from him. Once again, he gets to take ownership of the situation and have a say in the baby's life. If he's younger, snap a picture of him working in the nursery, frame it, and display it on the baby's dresser.

Registering for Baby Gifts. If you're registering, have your kid help you make a list of everything you need for the baby. If he's old enough, he could be in charge of setting up the registry online. Ask him to check the website a couple times a week, and provide you and New Love with an update of all the good things that have been purchased for the baby.

Baby Shower VIP. Chances are, a baby shower of some type is in your future. Make it multifunctional by giving Junior VIP guest status. From a specially decorated seat, complete with balloons and streamers, to a Future Big Brother/Big Sister T-shirt, there are many ways to make your kid feel special and part of the festivities.

If he's a little older, you can ask him to greet the relatives, or hand out game prizes to the winning guests. A younger kid will have fun helping you unwrap and show off the presents.

Preferred Hospital Guest. Let your kid know he gets to be the baby's first visitor at the hospital. Whether he's hanging out in the waiting room or at home with grandparents, make sure he's contacted first, and that the rest of the family is well aware that no one else gets to see the baby before your kid does.

Baby Photographer. A fun way to get Junior interacting with his new sibling is to give him photography duty. Well before the due date, either teach Junior how to operate your digital camera, if he's old enough, or buy him an indestructible kid's version. Let him get his feet wet by photographing his mom's expanding belly, the new nursery, and anything else he might want to photograph for the baby to see one day. Once the baby's born, let him go wild capturing every moment that you would otherwise be too tired, or too busy to get yourself.

Buy a special photo album that's just for Junior's photos. Make sure he takes a few self-portraits of him and his new sibling (where he turns the camera around and snaps), so pictures of both kids make it into the album. If he's into art, let him decorate the cover of the album and choose which photo to place on front.

While involving Junior in the baby fun is a great way to make him feel included and get him excited about a new sibling, you still may have to deal with some fallout that adding a new member to the family may cause.

"It's pretty hard to ask kids to feel something," Wish says. "You can't manufacture that. Some kids want to be the older sibling and take care of the baby. Others want to be left alone, yet know they haven't been forgotten about. You have to know your child."

Here are a few questions and comments you may encounter:

Are You Replacing Me? While this is one of those rare times when you can so booyah your kid with a straight-faced, "Yes, we've had enough of you leaving your dirty laundry on your bedroom floor and have indeed decided to replace you with a kid who listens," this is probably not the best occasion to poke fun at Junior.

Let your kid know you've had such an awesome experience raising him, you're hoping for a chance to not only do it again, but to give him an opportunity to share in that joy as well. It's also important for him to understand this is a chance for him to experience a sibling—someone he can grow up with and have as a friend forever. Or at least someone he can blame things on, possibly escaping a punishment as a result.

You're Creating a New Family, and I'm Part of the Old Family. Ah, the ol' "in with the new, out with the old" concern. Sure you can replace shoes or golf clubs like the worn ones meant nothing to you. And while you know you could never replace your first born, Junior needs reassurance he means more than an over-used possession.

Let Junior know he was your first—your original—baby. No matter who comes into your life, from a new baby to a new friend, you two are joined together forever, and nothing will ever change that. Have him think of the two of you as a team, navigating your every adventure together. Sometimes, something as simple as a code word or a secret handshake is enough for Junior to feel bonded to you, and secure about his place in your home.

A New Baby Means More Work For Me. While it's true your kid could end up with a few extra chores, make sure anything extra your kid does to help with the baby evens out in his weekly chores. (Or in some other, this-is-sort-of-worth-it way.)

Try not to deliver the "Doing Your Part" speech that, while true, isn't going to do much good if your kid is having trouble adjusting to the idea of a new baby in his life. Sure, all kids need to pull their weight, but at this potentially complex time, if your kid is going to spend more time cleaning, running errands, or whatever is useful at his particular age, it wouldn't hurt to sweeten the pot so he's encouraged to help out, as opposed to feeling used.

Consider upping his allowance during this time, or perhaps selecting a special gift you have wrapped and waiting to give him after you and the baby come home from the hospital. Showing you appreciate the extra effort will make a big difference to your kid.

15

Attending Events Together

*I*f since the divorce you haven't been in the same place at the same time with your ex—outside of quick kid exchanges—attending an event together may have you feeling apprehensive. Before you embark on this new adventure, first consider if the time is right.

Perhaps the break up is still too new for one or both of you. If so, that's okay. While having both of you attend a soccer game or the science fair would be nice for Junior, it's only nice if one of you isn't shooting daggers at the other from across the room. And you don't want one of you to spontaneously burst into tears in the middle of his piano recital. (Unless he's playing a really moving piece, of course.) If being in the same room—especially if one of you has moved on with someone new and said new person is also in attendance—simply hurts too much, then the time isn't right. Eventually it will be.

If you're both invited to an event, such as a wedding, and you don't feel ready to spend any amount of time with your ex, then sharing a table will definitely not be on your agenda. Wish suggests contacting the person who invited you ahead of time to discuss your concerns.

"If there's no way to avoid being seated at the same table, find out who else will be at your table, arrive early, and surround yourself with those people," Wish says. "If you and your ex make eye contact, nod, smile, and be cordial." She also suggests bringing recent pictures of your kid to give to your ex to warm up the atmosphere.

When it comes to events you have control over, create a schedule that allows you and your ex individual time with your kid. If Junior participates in a sport, then alternate attending games. If it's a dance recital or a spelling bee, maybe it's more important for one of you to attend than the other. A thoughtful thing to do—and you can be the one to start this—is to record the event and then send the recording to your ex. That way neither of you has to feel you completely missed an important moment for your kid.

In the Same Room with No Bloodshed. Once enough time has passed, or if you had a decent enough divorce that it's not a huge deal to be within a stone's throw of each other, then go about attending events together. Just don't attempt to hang shoulder-to-shoulder, become too familiar, or do anything that might warrant the evil eye from your ex or anyone on that side of the family.

Let's go with the example of a soccer game, since that's where I spend the most time with my ex, his wife, her son, and their extended family. When we first started attending games together—which was a couple of years after our divorce, since Noah was only three years old during the time of the breakup—I was already with Frank, but my ex wasn't in any type of serious relationship. I chose to go to a few games solo, to test the waters before inviting Frank to come along. That first game was … awkward. There's really no other way to put it. I think we both found it a little ridiculous to stand on opposite ends of the field and pretend we didn't know each other, so we stood together, with plenty of breathing room between us, naturally.

Morely says to make sure the custodial person—or whoever is in charge of managing the sports calendar—gives the other parent the schedule for the year, which makes that parent feel included and in the know. Then be the bigger person and contact your ex to find out if you'll both be in attendance and how you would like the situation handled.

"Explain that you want to sit together," she says. "Remind your ex that you're there for your child, and it won't look good to him if you're sitting on opposite sides of the field. Children know when things are awry between adults. So remember what your purpose is for that day."

The thing that's so nice about coming together at a sporting event is there's actually something to talk about. Or maybe not so much talk about as comment on from time to time. You'll still have quiet moments, but they're not those utterly uncomfortable lulls in the conversation where you can't think of a single appropriate thing to say. Junior passes the ball to a teammate and you can say, "Wow, he's really getting better at giving up the ball." Or, "Hey, did you see that? He didn't fall over that time." It's a great way to begin talking to each other again.

What was difficult for me was—having known my ex since we were 14 years old—I *wanted* to talk. Not long, convoluted heart-to-hearts or anything outlandish. I had been talking to him for *years*. I was used to it. So, of course, I could get too chatty too easily. Even today, after being divorced for nine years, I still talk too much to my ex. And I can tell when I do. His interest kind of drifts off, like when you tell a bad joke and your friend tries to chuckle for your sake, but it's totally half-hearted and you know you bombed it.

So start slow. Agree that both of you will attend the same event. If having a crowd of other cheering parents between you two makes the first few (or several) times easier, then so be it. Eventually, you'll have to get within speaking distance of each other. If your ex isn't making that move, then you need to be the one to do it. Arrive a little late, so your ex has a chance to claim a spot to watch the game. Casually stroll over to your ex, give a little smile, then stop close enough that you don't have to shout to one another, but not so close that you're invading personal space. Since the game has already started, you have a perfect opportunity to ask, "Is there a score yet?" Even if your ex only nods or manages an "Uh-uh," you made an exchange. Don't engage your ex again until there's a reason to. Use a goal, a good pass, a collision, or anything else reasonable to do with the game to make easygoing comments. If your ex ignores you, don't get upset. These things can take time. It's possible your ex may also be a little bit suspicious, wondering what you're up to. Don't take any bait, don't be sarcastic, don't do anything but make those easygoing comments when the situation allows. You may have to go about this for a few games, but sooner or later your ex will figure out you mean no harm, and have no ulterior motives.

Now, if you have a New Love and you bring New Love along to the game, do not, I repeat, do not act like you're loopy for New Love. Note: this rule even applies if you were cheated on and your ex moved on with that person. To build a good relationship with your ex, you have to take the high road. Don't flaunt New Love. Don't make out with New Love. Don't laugh hysterically at New Love's witticisms. Don't do anything to draw attention to yourself. It's totally fine to bring New Love; just behave like a mature adult. Yes, even if your ex is playing tonsil hockey in the grass with a significant other. Take the high road. And take deep, cleansing breaths while you're at it. There you go.

Time to Engage the Significant Other. If your ex's significant other and/or family members are present, this is definitely the time to engage those people. Even if you've never had any type of conversation with your ex's significant other before. And if that person has a kid in attendance? Even better. Does that kid look like the significant other? Mention it. Not in a sarcastic, back-handed compliment way, of course. It's "Wow, your son looks just like you!" or "Your daughter has your blue eyes, lucky girl." Not "Wow, your son looks just like you. Is he getting beat down in school yet?" or "Look at that! Your daughter has your lazy eye." There is nothing like a regularly occurring sporting event to break down the wall between you and your ex's significant other.

And that's your directive: break down the significant other's wall. If that person regularly attends the games, all the easier for you. Keep showing up at the games, actively engaging the significant other in a friendly, non-threatening, and non-overpowering way. Eventually, the significant other will engage, too. You may only get polite responses at first, but over time, the conversation will become more genuine. Even if you're not the biggest fan of your ex's significant other, if you truly give it a chance you'll probably find there's a thing or two you like about the person. You don't have to become best friends. You don't even have to be good friends. You simply want to be able to come together and have it be a pleasant—and possibly even fun—situation.

Now, if the significant other is cold toward you and refuses to engage, back off a little. But not altogether. Stay within that general vicinity of your ex and the significant other, and engage only once per game. Don't make your comment right at the start, either. Wait a bit and let the game get going. Let there be a reason to strike up a conversation. Once again, direct it to the significant other, not your ex. Keep it friendly. If you get nothing in return, don't act insulted or toss out an unkind remark under your breath. It won't be easy. And it may take an entire season of games. But the more restrained you are, the less of a threat you appear. Always keep in mind that the significant other may be intimidated or unsure of you (yes, even if your ex cheated on you with this person), or may think you have ulterior motives that aren't yet clear. You need to put in the time so the significant other sees you simply as your kid's mom, and not a threat.

If you don't seem to be getting anywhere with lessening the significant other's hostility toward you, another option might be to be kind to the significant other's kid, if there is one. Always try to connect with the significant other first, but if you're not seeing results, genuine kindness to the kid could help. Just don't be obvious about it. Don't try to become best friends with the kid, either. And whatever you do, don't offer anything to the kid without clearing it with the parent first. That's the quickest route to pissing off the significant other. Open a piece of gum (sugarless!) for yourself and offer a piece to the group. Shoot the significant other a quiet "Can Junior have gum?" You may get a firm no as your response, and that's fine, respect it. At another game, if you have your kid's soccer ball handy, you can drop it on the ground and move it around a bit with your foot, accidently rolling it in the direction of the significant other's kid. Then you can ask the kid to kick it back. These ideas for connection may seem inconsequential, but they do help to break the ice.

If you also have a kid in attendance, give yours something to bring along to the game that can be easily shared. You and the significant other may not currently be hitting it off, but that doesn't mean your kids can't. And they can be the key to get the two of you talking. Even a little.

When I first met my ex's stepkid, he was very young and very shy around me. I don't think he could fully wrap his head around me. Maybe it was weird for him that I was sitting next to his stepdad during Noah's karate practice, and he didn't know if that was okay or not. All I know is, he barely said a word to me. Even today, while we can goof around with each other, or gang up on Noah for a joke, there's still a little shyness on his part. However, put Frank in his vicinity, and everything changes. It's like watching two ten-year-old boys hanging together. They play soccer on the sidelines while Noah's in the middle of a game. Frank can tackle him and threaten him with a wedgie, and the kid eats it up. They're total buddies. It's not something I could have accomplished in that guy-understands-guy way. And I'm sure Frank, being an outsider—meaning not involved in the divorce—doesn't feel threatening in the least. That's where your New Love comes into play.

As the outsider, that person who doesn't pose a threat to your ex's new family, New Love is in a great position to establish a connection with your ex's significant other and stepkid. Explain your game plan to New Love. Ask for a helping hand in trying to establish a connection. And make sure nothing New Love does while chatting with the significant other comes off as flirting. Even the teeny-tiniest bit. The last thing you want to do here is piss off your ex and turn New Love into a seeming menace. Keep the plan to what you've been trying with the significant other: break down the wall by actively engaging in a friendly, non-threatening, and non-overpowering way.

If New Love starts making progress with the significant other and/or the stepkid, the next step is to bring you into the conversation. This is a team effort, so you and New Love should come up with an easy topic that New Love can start and you can be pulled into. It's 100 percent up to New Love to follow through with the plan, keeping it light and easy-going and not at all, well... planned. Once you've been pulled in, make your friendly contribution, then pull out of the conversation immediately. Go back to watching the game and let New Love keep the chatter going. Baby step. Next game, do it again, and stay in the conversation a little longer. Before you know it, the significant other's guard will be down and you can start your own conversations without needing an intermediary.

16

Don't Forget the In-Laws

Out of all the things that came out of my divorce, the one thing I never expected was the number of grandparents Noah would end up having. Eleven. That's right: eleven grandparents. And let's not forget his two great-grandparents. Both my ex's parents and Frank's parents are divorced and all of them have a significant other. Then add in my mom as well as my ex's wife's parents to the mix. Let me say for the record, that's a lot of presents for Noah at birthday time. And it's a lot to manage, too.

Imagine that birthday. With eleven grandparents (and two great-grandparents) living in an approximate thirty-mile radius, and all of them wanting to see Noah—between my ex and me, we could spend two weeks taking our kid around from party to party. And trying to schedule one or two big parties would be a nightmare, trying to ensure no one is left out of the festivities.

And then there are presents. We try hard not to spoil Noah, but the load of gifts he pulls in—not only from grandparents, but also from aunts and uncles and of course his parents, too—can throw a serious wrench into our non-indulgent wishes.

The same issues come up at all the major holidays. Everybody wants to see Noah, and even though I consider myself an excellent multi-tasker, something's got to give. But can you eliminate something—or someone—without risk of insult? Actually, yes you can.

Pick Your (Holiday) Battles. You and your ex need to create a one-year schedule for all holiday and birthdays, yours included. Obviously, you would get Junior on your birthday and Mother's Day if you're the mama, or Father's Day if you're the papa. Everything else you can either share or alternate, depending on how important it is to you. And it would be best if *everything* wasn't important to you.

Of course you'd like to have your kid at each and every holiday or special occasion, but the fact is, you're divorced with a kid, so like everything else you've encountered so far, you have to compromise. And if you're helpful to your ex, meaning giving the approval for Thanksgiving on the slopes with your ex, your ex's spouse, and your ex's parents, then you'll get the same consent when you want to spend spring break on the beach with Junior, New Love, and your extended family.

If you're both in town for a holiday, determine way ahead of time how you're going to split that day or series of days. For example, on Christmas Eve we always go to dinner at my aunt's home. It's a tradition we've followed for years and years. Not having Noah there would be unthinkable. So that's my night. Noah wakes up with us on Christmas morning, we make coffee and cinnamon rolls and open presents, and then Noah is generally off to his dad's by late morning for the rest of the day.

In the last few years, both my ex and I added travel into our Christmas holidays. My family takes off to Pennsylvania every other year for a much larger gathering of siblings and nieces and nephews. We only go for two nights, so Noah's entire holiday isn't spent with us, and then my ex and his family often leave a day or two after for a little getaway that incorporates New Year's Eve. Not having my kid for any part of a holiday wasn't the easiest thing to get used to. It feels just like you would think it would feel—like something's missing. But I knew it would have to be that way from time to time, otherwise I would never get to take him for a full holiday.

Morely says you have to turn what some people view almost as a death—not having your kid for a holiday—into a celebration.

"Prepare yourself for it ahead of time," she suggests. "Some people are in denial until the day it happens and then they're angry. Make sure you have your own celebration together, and when your child is away, make sure you still have a life."

This is a great time to get away so you're not sitting around the house, missing your kid. Go visit a new city or take in new attractions around your area. Have friends over (no kids for that get-together, please). As Morely says, "You can be alone, but don't be lonely."

Wish suggests dividing up the holidays into smaller pieces: Thanksgiving lunch, Thanksgiving dinner, Thanksgiving dessert, Thanksgiving on Friday. "Divide them into chunks of your day, or even courses of your meal," she says. "If all else fails, create your own. Put your Christmas tree up earlier and celebrate the week before. At least then you'll be the first one to give your kid a present someone else also bought for him."

Once you have your holiday schedule decided, then you can plan time with your in-laws. Consider working out a sub-schedule with them. Let's take the example of you having your kid Christmas Eve and Christmas morning. Let's say, worst-case scenario, there are four sets of parents, assuming your parents and New Love's parents are divorced and possibly with other people. The easiest thing you can do is have everyone come to you, since you have the most people to see. Of course that means a heck of a lot of entertaining on your part, but if you like that idea, then go for it. You can break it down into two gatherings by inviting your mom and significant other and New

Love's mom and significant other for one gathering, and your dad and significant other and New Love's dad and significant other for the other gathering. If you have the good fortune of everyone getting along, and they're agreeable, make it one giant party.

But if all the parents have their own sides of the family they get together with and they want you to be part of that as well, scheduling will be more complicated. Chances are you can't say yes to four parties in a day and a half—and you'd probably enjoy having time for an intimate gathering with just New Love and the kids. The only thing to do in this case is to have honest chats with your parents. Maybe you can celebrate with one group of parents the week before or the week after. Maybe one group comes to your house. Perhaps you can take your single parent with you to New Love's family home. Plan precisely, before you burn out and lose all your jolly. Find a way to enjoy the family time without feeling you're being pulled in ten different directions.

If you do need to appear at every family's home and it's impossible for your kid to attend and still have his time with his other parent, then so be it. He doesn't go to everything. This may be easier to orchestrate with New Love's parents rather than your mom or dad, so take advantage of those get-togethers to arrive minus a kid. Gather his presents and make sure he writes thank-you notes, possibly including snapshots of him opening or posing with the gifts.

Wish says usually one grandparent emerges as the neediest, who likes to call the shots. This is the one who won't be happy with the get-together planning unless it fits his or her schedule.

"You need to sit down with that person and say, 'What do you think is a good plan?' Sometimes, when you put these people in charge, they get flustered," Wish explains. "Because they're happiest when they're complaining. When you put them in charge of giving you advice—not in charge of the decisions, but the advice—you'd be surprised at how tame they become. They aren't craving power; they want to be recognized as important."

Determine Step-Grandparent Parameters. You may find when step-grandparents enter the picture you'll need to follow a few parameters so your kid's natural grandparents don't feel slighted by these newcomers.

Of course you want New Love's parents to bond with Junior, and your ex may feel the same way regarding the significant other's parents. They're part of the family now, and bringing them together for an event or a nice sit-down dinner is definitely warranted. However, if time with them means canceling or changing plans with the natural grandparents, feelings can easily be hurt.

You may feel slighted yourself if you miss an event or special occasion because your kid is off with his step-grandparents. I remember one time, while trying to plan a holiday schedule and all the get-togethers that went along with it, my ex wanted Noah for multiple family parties, including one with his wife's family. While I have zero issues about Noah spending time with her parents—they are awesome people and have always welcomed my kid as one of their own—it meant I couldn't have Noah with my immediate family for the actual holiday. That was a no-no for me. Just as I would never keep my kid from attending an event with his dad for a gathering with Frank's family, I expected the same. I stood firm on that point, and my ex ended up relenting. On many occasions Noah wasn't at a Christmas or Thanksgiving gathering with my in-laws because it conflicted with his time with his dad. You have to create these parameters together—and well ahead of time—so everyone can make the most of whatever time is available with your kid.

Step-grandparent parameters can also come up in regard to baby-sitting duty. My mom would cause me great bodily harm if an opportunity arose for her to have Noah for an overnight, and I dropped him off with my in-laws, instead. That's not to say Noah has never had a sleepover at any of his step-grandparents' homes. He has stayed with my ex's in-laws on a number of occasions, but they've been on his dad's scheduled days, not mine. Try to make concessions for your parents if you can. Over time, you can work in more visits with the step-grandparents.

Some parents are more laid back about sharing with the steps than others. Some may live too far away for babysitting, while others are never home when you need the help. And some may actually practice what they preached to you for years during your childhood about sharing nicely with others. Gauge the situation, keep the lines of communication open so you know how everyone feels, and take it from there.

Time to Re-bond (Somewhat) with Your Ex-In-Laws

If you haven't had a run-in yet with your ex-in-laws, or you have but it was distant and/or uncomfortable, this is a good time to take action. (Or at least consider the notion.)

You know what they say: In-laws—can't live with 'em, can't kill 'em. So imagine the fun when your in-laws become your ex-in-laws. If you never liked them, well, lucky you! They're not your in-laws anymore. If you adored them, then you didn't just lose a spouse when you divorced, you lost family. Either way, since you and your ex have a kid together, your in-laws will never fully exit your life, unless they live on a remote desert island with no plans to reconnect with society. (Then, *really* lucky you.)

I, unfortunately, loved my in-laws. My mother-in-law was far more than family. She had become one of my best friends. Needless to say, when I left her son, I left her, too. And we both suffered from that loss.

What I wanted was to get through the divorce, call my ex-mother-in-law, and make a date for a movie. Instead I got an email from her letting me know I'd broken her heart. I had never experienced such emotional distress from a breakup, even when I was the one getting dumped by someone I still wanted to be with. And it was over my ex-mother-in-law.

Needless to say, we didn't talk or see each other for a long time.

By the time we finally came face-to-face at a soccer game, enough time had passed that we felt more comfortable with one another. We started with cordial smiles, no talking. We sat with multiple people between us. Like I said, it could have been worse.

Over the next two years I saw her from time to time at a game or one of Noah's concerts, and the ice slowly melted. We transitioned from cordial smiles to making small talk—very small—and before I knew it we were back to discussing books and movies, and calling each other to make transportation arrangements for Noah. Did we become best friends again? No. But that wasn't because we no longer had as much in common or no longer found each other interesting and fun to chat with. I think we both realized such a relationship just wasn't appropriate. How would my ex have felt if he knew his mom and I were hanging out, behaving like mother-in-law and daughter-in-law again? How would his new wife feel? Would they wonder if we were talking about them? If it was me, I would wonder. And even if no one actually was talking about me, I still wouldn't like the feeling. So I enjoy her company at the soccer games and try not to talk too much, out of respect for my ex's wife. It sucks a little, but I'm grateful to have her back in my life, even in a limited way.

"One of the most difficult things about breaking off a marriage is that all your family ties are broken," Haltzman says. "Nonetheless, many people find they continue to have a positive relationship with their in-laws. But remember not to step on your ex's toes during relationships you maintain with your ex in-laws."

Haltzman adds that reminding your ex-in-laws you continue to maintain a bond with them through the kids is a subtle way of letting them know they're still part of your family and encourage them to see the benefit of maintaining a positive relationship with you. "Having a positive relationship with people who are still involved in your life sends an important message to your children that they're part of a family."

Morely adds that often it's your ex-in-laws who won't let go of your relationship—and that's okay to some degree.

"You can remain friends, but there must be boundaries," she says. "You shouldn't be over there every day, but you can have lunch every now and then. Make it clear to them you don't want to interfere in your ex's life and you wish to respect both your ex and your ex's significant other. But don't be afraid to keep in touch."

17

*When One Parent
Won't Play Nice*

$\mathcal{Y}$ou may be wondering when you can expect to
see results from all the tips and advice you learned from this book.
That's a good question. Unfortunately, the answer depends on your
state of mind as well as your ex's attitude. If you had a relatively
smooth, mutually agreed upon divorce, you'll be able to converse
more naturally and have fewer issues with parenting or attending an
event together. But that's the best-case scenario. Divorce is seldom
that neat and tidy.

Even if the divorce was one-sided, reaching a decent place where
you can at least email back and forth to handle scheduling or kid
concerns can happen relatively soon—as long as the person who was
left can let go of the marriage and the emotions, or at least actively
work on it. Being able to pick up the pieces and move on to the
next chapter in life—whatever that may be—makes a huge difference
when it comes to dealing with your ex in a respectful and helpful way.
That doesn't mean you and your ex will be sitting in the same row

for your kid's dance recital—you may need more time to reach that point. That's okay. The ability to parent together will start the process in the right direction. Everything else can happen in its own time.

But what if your ex can't let go? What if the bitterness won't dissipate? And (gasp) what if *you're* the one who keeps refusing to play nice and co-parent with your ex? Let's not forget, just because you're reading this book doesn't necessarily mean you've figured out your end of things, and are now focused on helping your ex do the same. You may be the bitter one. You may be the one having trouble moving on. Well, this chapter is for everyone who still has significant work to do before reaching that one big happy family scenario. (Which you *will* ultimately get to.)

First, Hone In On the Why. No matter which of you has trouble playing nice or co-parenting, before you can hope to fix a problem you need to know why it's happening.

"Commonly, when one spouse feels bitter or upset about the loss of another spouse, that person holds onto that anger. Often it ends up eroding any hope of a positive relationship between the two ex-partners," Haltzman says. "The less bitter partner, the one who wants to move on and forget the anger, often feels compelled to demand the more bitter partner let go of these negative feelings, recognizing it isn't helping anything. However, for many people who remain bitter or angry, holding onto these negative emotions is a way of clinging to the relationship—they're afraid if they let go of the bitterness they'll have nothing left."

Let's say the issue is with you. Maybe your ex not only left you for another person, but that relationship was going on for the last two years of your marriage. And when your ex left, also left behind was your kid, who no longer figured into your ex's grand scheme with the significant other. And you just found out they're planning to get married while the ink is still drying on your divorce papers.

That could sure make a person feel pissy, eh?

Of course it could! This could make you mad, in the crazy sense, potentially wandering the alleys barefoot with a fifth of Jack Daniels stashed in each of your coat pockets. You could be fervently Googling the significant other, looking for any ammunition to … well, you have no idea what it would be for, but dammit, you want ammunition! You could easily spend a whole heck of a lot of time dwelling on, and wallowing in, your predicament. And you have every right in the world to feel that way. So then, if one day you receive an email asking you to switch Junior's days so your ex and the significant other can attend a swanky party, what might be your swift reply? Probably a rousing, "Hell no!" And maybe in parenthesis you would add, "Good luck getting a babysitter with such short notice, dumbass!"

What's that going to get you? Two seconds of euphoria followed by months of fallout.

Would that do anything to better your world? Of course not. And, if you take a few moments to reflect on it, you may realize such antics could, in fact, harm Junior, even if that's not your intention. Imagine you were supposed to take your kid to an event he had been talking about nonstop for weeks, but then something came up at work and you were no longer able to do it. You send your ex an email asking for help so Junior can still attend the event. And your ex retaliates against your earlier behavior by refusing to switch the schedule. Are you willing to risk rocking the co-parenting boat because you couldn't keep the bitterness out of your communications? Too often, when exes fight—or try to harm one another—the one who suffers the most is your kid. Always keep that in mind.

So to alleviate that animosity and make the situation better for everyone, you have to name the why. Why are you so resentful? Is it because you were left behind? Is it because the significant other is fifteen pounds lighter than you? Is it because you now feel replaceable? Is it because you feel like an idiot for trusting someone your best friend was never crazy about? (And you've already heard, "I told you so" three dozen times?) There could be more than one reason. You may already know the reason, without the need for deep, meaningful reflection. But you have to come to terms with the why, so you can move past it.

If your ex is the one harboring bitterness and inconveniently won't speak to you in more than one-word hisses, how in the world are you supposed to figure out the issue and break through it?

"Your best chance at understanding the why of your ex's ongoing anger is to genuinely attempt to listen—without defending yourself, explaining, or correcting—to exactly what your ex-partner is concerned about," Haltzman says. "Then, once you understand, offer a heartfelt apology for any harm you may have done. This may not cure the situation, but it might help you to understand, and may open new channels of communication for the future."

You also need to be honest with yourself. Even if you are absolutely certain you did nothing warranting an apology to your ex, it's amazing the affect the words "I'm sorry" can have on another person. Consider one important reason to say it, even if you don't want to (or need to). It can help the healing, which means it can help your kid.

Maybe you did the cheating, which resulted in your ex doing the leaving. Maybe you did the walking away, believing it was obvious the marriage was bad, bad, bad, yet your ex was caught completely off-guard, assuming everything was hunky dory. Or at least not so bad that you two couldn't work through your issues. Ask yourself, why did the marriage end? What was your role? How can you use that information to improve the current situation?

Second, Do Your Best to Reach Out. Do you remember the letter to your ex that was suggested in Chapter One by Wish? If you didn't think it necessary to write one at the beginning of the book, yet you're still having trouble getting your ex to communicate without using four-letter words, maybe you should rethink the letter. This would definitely be the right time to write.

If you did send your ex the letter, but have yet to feel you've made headway because of it, consider writing another. But only after you've taken the time to contemplate potential reasons that might explain your ex's bad feelings towards you. Taking ownership of your contribution to the divorce will move you much farther than going the easy route and blaming everything on your ex.

Did you just swear at me?

Even if your spouse left you, and you didn't do anything obvious, such as an affair, abuse, or anything illegal to cause that person to desert the marriage, if you let yourself take the proverbial walk down memory lane, you may find you played a larger role than you realized. Did you have doubts you were marrying the right person, yet went ahead with the marriage anyway? Did you fight all the time when you were dating and then were surprised when, after getting married, the fighting continued, and possibly grew worse? Did you regularly spend over your budget, causing you both financial troubles? Did you rarely spend money, keeping an eagle eye on every penny so it wasn't much fun to contemplate a vacation? Did you clam up every time your feelings came into question? Did you shout more often than you talked? While your actions didn't directly bring the marriage to an end, perhaps they aided the process. People usually get divorced for more than one simple, easy-to-define reason. There's a good chance that somehow, some way, you were a cog on the big wheel that spun your marriage to the point of no return.

What, you're *still* swearing at me?

Okay, if you were the epitome of the perfect spouse, who gave far more than you ever took, then fine: your ex sucks and it's not on you.

Why do I keep going on about this?

Because, if you want to cut through the crap and turn the person who isn't playing nice into a team player—a person who could, in fact, be you (don't hit me!)—then you have be honest about all this junk.

So then, back to that letter. Write one now—or—write another one now. Be honest and heartfelt. Don't talk about why things went wrong. Don't go into details. Apologize that things turned out the way they did. Express your respect for your ex. Note that you would very much like for you and your ex to co-parent in a way that's best for Junior and also allows you both to be relevant in your kid's life. It may suck to write such a letter, but if it gets you positive results with your ex, isn't it worth doing?

Third, Book a Series of Counseling Sessions. Although you may be positive your ex's hard feelings and bad vibes aren't directly related to you, see a psychologist, a counselor, a family therapist— whatever works for you—for at least a few weeks. Even if you only go one day a week for a month, this isn't a large investment of time and the cost isn't offensive. (Have you seen the bill after a couple of bottles and a cheese platter at a good wine bar?) In fact, many health insurance plans cover a set number of counseling sessions per year.

Why should you see a therapist if it's not about you? Because anything that involves or affects your kid *is* about you. You may not be a fan of therapy; you may find it uncomfortable and tedious, but if there's a chance you'll benefit Junior by seeing someone, then you owe it to yourself to try this.

A therapist can help you see things you may not recognize on your own. Or, help you see things from a different point of view: your ex's. Your kid's, too. Any way you look at it, a little therapy can benefit you a lot. And, your ex may be pleased to know you're going to therapy in hopes of learning how to positively co-parent together. Sometimes just knowing another person has taken a big (uncomfortable) step to improve a bad situation can, in itself, improve that situation.

Fourth, Give Your Ex More Time to Come Around. Some people take a long time to bounce back from tragedy. And divorce can be tragic. This is a life-changing event that can break you like you've never been broken before, especially if you weren't expecting it. Show empathy for your ex. Let kindness be your rule. The healing process may take a year or two. But if you stay the course, during that time you will see improvements, even if they're only slight changes at first. Be patient.

"No solution happens quickly, and there's no simple fix for this," Haltzman says. "To the greatest extent possible, the partner who wishes to improve the relationship should inject hope, caring, gratitude, and positivity into all interactions with the ex. People find it hard to sustain high levels of anger with a gracious, loving person. In most cases, the degree of hostility will eventually fade."

Morely suggests using "I" messages when you aren't getting anywhere with your ex. "I'd really like to talk with you. I'm concerned that when our child sees us together, he sees anger. I need your help with this. I'm not willing to take the disrespect or anger. I'm not going to tolerate this in my house or in front of my son."

You have to begin to control the areas you can control. Continue to be the bigger person. Show your ex that, either way, you're moving forward with your life.

Wish advises trying the positive techniques more than once, but don't go on forever. "I measure the success of a technique in half years. Six months. After that, then I wouldn't recommend trying so hard. Be civil. Be warm. Say thank you when it's appropriate, but stop trying so hard."

For some people, finding a new love finally helps them deal amicably with the old love. So be extra supportive if your ex finally does show up to a soccer game with a significant other. Don't offer to pay for their honeymoon, but do be welcoming. When that time comes, go back and reread chapters eight and eleven—heck, feel free to create traveling index cards, if you need them. Do whatever it takes on your end to keep your ex and that significant other swooning for each other.

Wish says in addition to falling in love again, another common turning point for a bitter ex is having your kid reach an age where the ex can better relate to him. "If that parent can forge a special activity with the child, it makes them feel special," she says. "Plus, you can be encouraging by saying, 'Junior really loved being with you; you did a great job.' That gives you concrete reasons to say thank you."

18

If You're Ready to Live On a Compound

*W*hen I first met Frank, I told him flat out I would never move out of the area, so if leaving town was in his future plans, I shouldn't be part of those plans. I knew I'd never move away, because I would never separate Noah from his dad.

The situation is different if you have sole custody because your ex is locked up in the pokey for a felony, or is an alcoholic who refuses to get help. Then you might want to move as far away as possible, or at least far enough so you don't have constant run-ins or read about your ex's latest escapades in the police blotter of the local paper.

Noah's dad is nothing like that. He's a good dad and a great influence on his son. They like spending time together, and I like co-parenting with him. Why would I ever move Noah away from that?

While I would never have expected it when we first divorced, the four parents get along so well that at one point I suggested to my ex we should all move to a compound in Florida and take our parents with us as well. I was only half-joking. I didn't want to share a house, or even a backyard, but I sure could have lived with all of us in close proximity to each other where a short walk would get us to anyone's house. Babysitting would be a cinch. If Noah forgot a school book at his dad's house and he was with me for the night, he could run over there and be back in five minutes. The compound would make for a convenient life.

My ex had a good chuckle over my suggestion, but I know in my heart we could actually make a scenario like that happen. That's how good it has become over the years. They would be like those good neighbors you can always count on. You may not become best friends with them, but you're glad to know they're nearby.

My friend Janis has a funny story about attending a high school reunion where she and her husband sat with her ex and his girlfriend. Janis and her ex were seated next to each other and everyone was chatting back and forth and having a good time. As former classmates passed their table, many stopped to marvel at what they thought were childhood sweethearts still together after all these years. "It's a funny story we love to tell," she says, "having to tell everyone congratulating us, 'No, we've been divorced for years.'"

My friend Leslie had such a great relationship with ex number one and his family that they used to meet at their son's summer camp each year on Visiting Day to spend time together.

"We would go canoeing, have wine, and lovely dinners. It was great," she says. "We called ourselves the functional-dysfunctional family."

While everyone may not reach the level of these friendly and positive post-divorce situations, you will find a level both you and your ex can deal with. Maybe you're not chit-chatty at the soccer game, but you can sit by each other. Perhaps you prefer not to sit at the same table at your son's wedding, but you can share a laugh over your bad moves on the dance floor. This is all about finding *your* version of one big happy family, not mine.

We see so many horrible depictions of divorce on TV every day. Whether it's real on the evening news, or fictional on every soap opera and prime-time drama, we're conditioned to assume that divorce equals disaster. A never-ending disaster. Quite simply, what media outlet revels in showcasing a *good* divorce? Where's the fun in that? An amicable relationship after divorce may create boring television—but that doesn't mean it doesn't exist.

Divorce rates are still around the 50 percent mark. I'm guessing 100 percent of those people are not spending their remaining days on the planet feeling angry and resentful. That means people *do* get over divorce. They may not be buddy-buddy with the exes, but they move on to create the next chapter of their lives. It's also true that some people never let themselves stop feeling angry and, sadly, will carry bitter feelings all the way to the grave.

My friend Janis can't comprehend holding onto such negative feelings. "The bitterness and the anger and the why me—some people never get beyond it," she says. "What a waste. Personally, those fifteen years I had as a single person, with all the ups and downs, were the best growing years ever. I liked myself better after those years of doing it on my own."

Get Ready to Recount. If you've followed the advice and used the tips in this book, and made positive strides in co-parenting with your ex, I ask you to end this chapter by going forth and showing other people who are in process of divorce or are newly divorced that, with enough effort and time (and kindness!), they too can co-parent without killing each other. Maybe they'll even become friends again.

"My husband and I broadcast the fact that we welcome our daughter's mother over for Mother's Day and Thanksgiving," Wish says. "Our relationship gives hope to people who are going through divorce. For some, it gives them an opportunity to think about possibly needing to change. For others it's a relief to hear how well things can work out."

People need to see examples of what's possible. I hope I've been your good example throughout this book. Now you get to be the good example. Make the most of it!

Available from NorlightsPress and fine booksellers everywhere

Toll free: 888-558-4354   **Online:** www.norlightspress.com
Shipping Info: Add $2.95 - first item and $1.00 for each additional item

Name _____

Address _____

Daytime Phone _____

E-mail _____

No. Copies	Title	Price (each)	Total Cost

	Subtotal	
	Shipping	
	Total	

Payment by (circle one):
   Check   Visa   Mastercard   Discover   Am Express

Card number_____3 digit code_____

Exp.date_____ Signature_____

Mailing Address:
2323 S.R. 252
Martinsville, IN 46151

Sign up to receive our catalogue at
www.norlightspress.com

21917237R00097

Made in the USA
San Bernardino, CA
07 January 2019